How to Manage
One Million Dollars
or Less

How to Manage One Million Dollars or Less

COMPILED & EDITED BY BRIAN MAST

Bridge-Logos *Publishers*

Gainesville, Florida 32614 USA

How to Manage One Million Dollars or Less
Edited by Brian Mast
Copyright © 2000 by Bridge-Logos Publishers
Library of Congress Catalog Card Number: 00-107093
International Standard Book Number: 0-88270-796-5

Published by:
Bridge-Logos *Publishers*
P.O. Box 141630
Gainesville, Florida 32614
http://www.bridgelogos.com

Acknowledgments

On behalf of every reader, I thank the authors who contributed to make this book a success. Their combined years of experience, of which portions were compressed to fit within these pages, is truly staggering and beyond description. It will pay (literally) to give them not only our respect, but also our attention.

And as equally important, thank you to all the authors' spouses who gave their mates room enough to learn, fail, and succeed. The end result has brought benefit to us all. Thank you!

Special thanks also to Georgina Chong-You for her editorial help, and to Bridge-Logos Publishers for the platform from which these individuals are given voice.

Contents

Saving With a Purpose

Investing for the Future

Making Money—You Can Start Your Own Business

Managing Your Business

Business Reference Section

Preface

Money—while some never mention it, others talk of nothing else. From fanciful dreams of winning a lottery to fretful possibilities of losing a multi-million dollar portfolio, the issue of money and management is here to stay.

For each of us, our financial knowledge is simply the result of what we have learned or experienced over time. Our financial instructors have been our parents, professors, bosses, mentors, pastors, and friends. We go through life building upon this foundation, or lack of foundation, whether we are consciously aware of it or not.

Regardless of how we rate our current knowledge, there is always room for improvement. The individual with no money has much room to grow, as does the individual who has more wealth and information than he knows what to do with. How is this possible?

Because money is like a tool in the hands of a builder, wealth has no power to construct anything beyond the wishes of its designer. That is why people who suddenly become wealthy seldom build anything that lasts for more than a few short years. Their lack of foundation proved to be their own downfall, and they often end up in a worse state than before.

> Our financial instructors have been our parents, professors, bosses, mentors, pastors, and friends. Good or bad, that is what we have.

In today's age, and in many well-meaning circles, the proper understanding and management of money has become so misshapen that this generation (and the next) are in for a real fight. Presently, debt is not only expected, it is normal, yet it strangles people and businesses every year by the thousands. Countless careers, dreams and marriages are destroyed over debt, yet lending institutions continue to make the options more appealing. Something is wrong, and for many, their foundation of financial knowledge is sinking.

It is upon this quest for a solid financial foundation that we turn our attention.

People are always asking: How can I get more? How much is enough? Is there such a thing as good debt? Does money equal success? How much insurance do I need? How can I get a raise? What happens to the money I make? How much do I need to retire?

The questions are endless, but questions require answers, which in turn implies a lack of knowledge. That is what this book is all about—finding answers that will be of practical benefit to each of us, and to those we in turn will instruct.

Most, if not all, of the authors within these pages spent years of effort, believing and waiting for what they practiced and hoped for to come to pass. From debt reduction to estate planning and from corporate decisions to personal money management, they not only learned the hard way and questioned what they stood for, but some even wished to quit along the way. Instead, they chose to persevere, and for our mutual and present benefit. Following every principle will not bring instant success. Similarly, agreeing with every author is not a prerequisite for

From the novice to the expert, the only limit to our financial freedom is ourselves.

increased wealth, but due diligence must be carried out before any principle can be discounted.

In addition, these principles are not bound by any individual's current financial standing. From the novice to the expert, the only limit to our financial freedom is ourselves.

In all of this, the bottom line remains the same: each of us begins where the last person left off. The combined insight, knowledge and experience of these authors is ours for the taking.

Brian Mast
Editor

I
What God Expects of Your Money

1

The way it ought to be

Finding and implementing the order—and blessing—of God.

by George A. Brantley

There is an order by which God wants to bless every person on the face of the earth, regardless of race, education, status, age, etc. His blessing, unlike winning a lottery, is for everyone and will continue for generations to come.

Finding the order of God is not that difficult, it's the implementing part that is the most challenging.

Some may say, "But you don't understand where I came from" or "You don't know what my family did." To be honest, I would compare my past (bad habits, family misfortunes, lack of education, limited future, etc.) with anybody's. We can all claim to be victims of something in our past, but God has made provision for us.

Finding God's order for your life isn't that difficult. It's implementing it that's the most challenging. That consists of hearing, receiving, and obeying the Word of the Lord, then proving that Word in your life. If you don't faint or quit, in due season you'll witness the promise of God coming to pass. It's His promise, and He's faithful to all His promises and loving toward all He has made (Psalms 145:13b).

Blessing does not necessarily mean more money.

When people think of blessing, money most often comes to mind. In this important area, we each need to prove the faithfulness of God in our lives. To prove the faithfulness of God, we must diligently seek after Him. Then we will have the opportunity to see His Word come to pass. No big hope, exciting promise, anointing oil, or prophetic Word will ever override God's system: order first, blessing second.

His order—your order

The natural question is, "Where do I begin?" God starts with what we have and are willing to give back to Him. He uses what we are willing to prove Him with: our money, our time, our home, our family, etc. The basis of order and blessing is what we do with what we have.

His blessing doesn't automatically mean riches. I know scores of rich people who are miserable. In fact, most of these rich people are not being blessed; they just happen to have a lot of money. It isn't about getting rich, but about being blessed. God has a way of blessing everything we touch and are involved in, from our home to our work, from our kids to our car- and through it all, He is glorified.

Similarly, it is inaccurate to measure God's promises and faithfulness according to someone's personal time schedule. Everything, including all wealth, belongs to God, and just because some folks are lacking now doesn't mean God has no financial blessing intended for them.

4

Initial key to God's order and blessing

The initial key to promoting order and blessing in your life is learning what God has in store for you, then lining up with it. God's intent is that His blessings will overtake you (Deuteronomy 28:2). If the blessing overtakes you, then it follows that you will not have to pursue it, go looking for it, or try to make it happen.

This may require a major shift in our thinking. We need to come to a place in our lives where we don't worry about money because all our needs are being met in Christ Jesus (that, too, is a promise of God--Phillipians 4:19). We also need to recognize that we can't do anything to force a change or to open the avenue of blessing that God has in store for us. It's as if the door has one handle and one key hole, and both are on the inside. Interestingly enough, we each possess the key to open the door, but we don't have the power to open it ourselves. God opens the door with our key, which is the tithes and offerings.

The Key

Learn what God has in store for you, then line up with that Word.

Why tithes and offerings are important

What is it about our tithes and offerings that is so important? The answer is simple: *obedience*. God's desire is that all of His children will be blessed, but if we don't obey, we are robbing God and may therefore experience misfortunes instead of blessings (see Malachi 3).

God's established order for blessing is not only available to everyone, but it is equally accessible by all. The only thing that limits Him is our disobedience in giving tithes and offerings.

The tithe is the first and the best tenth of our income. It goes to fund the ministry that God has appointed. Anything given beyond that is an offering, but that is like going to our mortgage company or landlord and saying, "I baked you a fresh chocolate cake. It's right out of the oven and still warm. Do you like it?"

The paying of the tithe, at its deepest sense, is a measure of our heart toward God.

The owner, if he is patient, would most likely say, "Look, I appreciate the cake, but until you pay your mortgage, I don't want it. You either have to pay up, or move out." Many people try to give extra or do Christian things to earn brownie points with God. I'm sorry, but it won't work. We can't please God if we don't pay our tithes. In a deepe sense, the paying of the tithe is a measure of our heart toward God.

Admittedly, paying tithes and giving offerings won't bring about instant success. Any farmer who plants seed expects it to grow and return in a multiplied state, but not by tomorrow morning! The same principle of seed time and harvest applies to tithes and offerings. The rewards of obedience or disobedience take time to run their course.

His blessing—intended for you

Walking in God's order will bring more blessing than you could ever imagine in every area of your life- spiritually, mentally, physically, emotionally, materially. But what about money- how does this affect your personal finances?

To begin with, God's order can get you out of debt. How? By your faithfully paying tithes and giving offerings. It may seem simplistic, but I have personally given my way out of debt and proven God's faithfulness in this area, even if it didn't make sense mathematically or logically.

Like most people, I have had to learn the hard way. Twenty years ago, my wife stuck her finger in my chest and said with spiritual discernment, "Have you been robbing God?" We were newly-married and we both worked. We had a little apartment, one small car, and no kids. So all our bills should have easily been covered each month, but they weren't.

The problem was that I was paying tithes when I felt we could afford it. I was guilty, and we both knew it, but from that moment until this, I have never robbed God again. The resulting blessing in our lives is indescribable.

Living within our means

Though faithfully sowing good seed by paying tithes and giving offerings are vitally important to walking in God's order and blessing, they are not everything. In addition, we must do something that many believe to be impossible in this day and age: we must live within our means.

We have to break the curse of being in debt, or that will be the only thing our children's children will inherit.

For most of us, living within our means will require us to stop buying on credit. Let's be honest. When faced with an emergency, the natural response is to immediately whip out a credit card. Within no time, our 12 credit cards have gotten us into a very difficult position.

Individually we must reach a point where we say, "If I don't have the money today, I'm not buying it." We have to break the habit of being in debt, or that will be the only thing our children's children will inherit.

As a nation, we in the United States owe more than five trillion dollars. The question isn't how we got there, but how we will get out! The sad thing is that the majority of the new generation, whether in college or in high school, are already in debt, sometimes to the point of suicide. Unless we start applying God's principles of order to our lives now, we will have nothing to pass on.

In addition to living within our means, we must begin to declare that we are not living for ourselves any longer. You no doubt have seen the bumper sticker that says, "I'm spending my grandchildren's inheritance." If that is the condition of our hearts, we're in big trouble. By living in a way that prepares for the next generation, we're establishing God's order in our lives that will result in our children being blessed.

Seven steps toward order and blessing

1. Line up with the Word of the Lord
2. Pay your tithes
3. Be rich toward the ministry (offerings)
4. Be faithful to what God has called you to do
5. Live within your means
6. Don't get into debt
7. Set goals and be disciplined

Therefore, we not only need to bring our finances into order, but also our homes, our habits, and our families. Instead of training our children to purchase what they can't afford (after all, they only do what their parents do), we must establish in them the order that will bring God's blessing.

Begin to set goals

As we live within our means, the natural next step will be to begin to set goals. You are to be the lender instead of the borrower (Deuteronomy 28:12b). If you are in debt or wondering how to save for your children's children, ask God to give you a plan and seek wise council. Then, with all diligence, begin to walk that out. You will eventually attain your goal, and though it may take time, the accompanying blessings will be worth the effort.

Best kept financial secret of all time: live within your means.

When it is all said and done, every one of us will stand alone before God and give an account of our lives. Prove God with your finances. It doesn't matter if it takes you five, ten or twenty years, His promise is still for your blessing. Then, teach your children and your children's children to do the same. After all, isn't that the way it ought to be?

(George A. Brantley is Senior Pastor and Apostle at The Rock of Gainesville, a large and dynamic church in North Central Florida. He and his wife, Suzanne, have made a life-time commitment to ministry in Gainesville, where they reside with their three sons.)

2

The Three Tithes and Their Uses

**Understanding what God wants, and
how it benefits you.**

by F. Nolan Ball

In today's trading, the United States dollar is generally recognized as the basic monetary unit. This in turn gives stability, order, and confidence to the national and international exchange of goods and services. Similarly, the Kingdom of God has its own monetary unit of measure that provides stability and order. This unit is the tithe.

The basic meaning of tithe is "one-tenth," but the Scripture enlarges upon this basic meaning so that whenever the term is used, it is not just any one-tenth, but it is the "first and the best" tenth (Numbers 18:12).

The tithe is the rent we owe God.

In fact, the Lord makes it very clear that we can neither substitute the inferior for the best nor offer to God what is left over, after everything else has been taken care of. Any variation from this rule is an offering of dishonor and cursing—not of honor and blessing.

Paying rent to God

Those who use lands or buildings that are owned by others are expected to pay rent. In the same manner, because the earth is the Lord's (Psalm 24:1), all who use God's earth and its resources owe God, the lawful owner, rent. And God has already established that the tithe, one-tenth of the income a person receives, belongs to Him.

In a very real sense, the tithe is rent money, and therefore any person, not just the believer, who does not tithe is a thief and a robber. According to Leviticus 27:30, the tithe is holy because it belongs to the Lord; therefore, anyone who treats the tithe with anything less than respect is showing contempt for holy things and is incurring a curse.

In establishing the tithes and their regulations, God established financial support for three areas of society that would surely come up last if special provisions were not made for them, and they do come up last wherever the Biblical instructions are not followed, either because of ignorance or disobedience.

The three tithes:

#1-for the ministry
#2-for the family
#3-for the poor

These three areas are: the ministry, the family, and the poor. You can be sure that God's priorities are correct, but they are almost always 180 degrees off-line with the worldly system of priorities.

The Bible actually speaks of three tithes, and unless all three are properly understood, it is likely that what is said about the second and third tithe will be applied to the first, thus causing confusion and limiting the intended blessing.

First tithe—for the ministry

Not only is the purpose of the first tithe to honor God and acknowledge His ownership of the earth, but it is to support and provide for those whom God has called into full-time ministry. Numbers 18:21 makes it plain, "Behold, I have given the children of Levi all the tithes in Israel as an inheritance in return for the work which they perform, the work of the tabernacle of meeting."

Lack of money, either genuine or perceived, is a common killer of marriages.

In today's terms, an individual called into the five-fold ministry should only have to "hold down" one job, and that being to accomplish God's specific calling. When the full first tithe is received, other means of employment are not only unnecessary, they are unacceptable.

No societal group is more important to God than His Church, and no other agency does as much to shape a society. History will show that where there has been no church, or a weak and ineffective church, other forces have been able to produce a society without the strong moral fiber that can save a society from crumbling from within, or from being destroyed from without.

On the other hand, when the church is healthy and its voice is prophetic, it will always produce enough "salt and light" to make its society strong and preserve all the other component parts of that society: government, education, family, economy, etc.

To play the role that it is intended to, the church must be well cared for financially, and its financial strength must come from its active members. A church lacking in financial resources simply lacks the ability to release those of the five-fold ministry to prayer and the ministry of the Word, and acquire and maintain the lands, facilities, and equipment necessary to carry out its total mission.

I believe there is nothing else quite as deserving of financial support as the five-fold ministry. For this reason, God ordained that those whom He called into the ministry should be supported by the first tithe.

Second tithe—for the family

Historians and sociologists have repeatedly called attention to the importance of family life. Strong families produce strong cultures and societies, but once the family unit is weakened to any significant degree, there will be a corresponding loss of strength in the society.

Admittedly, there are countless forces that work independently or together to gnaw away at the inner strength of the family unit. Almost everyone acknowledges that one of the most prevalent and potent of destructive forces is divorce. And what brings about divorce? What has the power of turning lovers into bitter enemies? The one factor generally recognized as being predominant is money.

Occasionally an abundance of money coupled with worldly (non-biblical) values leads to a lifestyle that may eventuate in a destroyed marriage, but most often, it is not an abundance of money, but a lack, either genuine or perceived, that creates the problems. Therefore, God, knowing the necessity of strong family life for a strong society and knowing the necessity of a financial base for a strong family, from the very beginning put family financial planning second only to His interest in financial support for the ministry.

Tithing to one's self ought to take priority over the giving of offerings.

14

Tithing to ourselves

God teaches throughout the Bible the importance of tithing to ourselves as well as tithing to the ministry. Deuteronomy 12: 5-21 describes how the children of Israel were to travel to a location to offer their tithes, sacrifices, and offerings. Once there, they were to celebrate and enjoy these offerings, all in the presence of the Lord.

When Israel entered the Promised Land, God chose Jerusalem to be the place of worship where every man, including his family and servants, would observe and celebrate the various holy days with their accompanying feasts and sacrifice offerings.

Second only to God, your family is the most important part of your life!

Anyone who has taken a trip of any distance knows that living away from home, spending nights in hotels and eating in restaurants, becomes very expensive very quickly. Of course, God knew this when He gave the instruction to travel to Jerusalem for those specified holy days, and perhaps that is the primary reason each man was taught to tithe to himself. God never wanted a man to find it necessary to say to his family, "I am sorry, but we cannot afford to go to Jerusalem to worship God this year." Once that began happening, the nation would begin to experience a deterioration of the quality of life in the family, in the "church," and in the nation.

Taking time off from work is a step of faith. Normally, when a man is away from his farm, business, or profession, his income is diminished or completely eliminated during that time and for a period of time afterward.

Keeping priorities in order

Requiring the people to take time and travel as a family to Jerusalem had several positive results. Among other things, it helped a man keep his priorities in order. While work was important, it was never permitted to override the importance of a man's worship and his relationship with his family. Regular attendance at the specified feasts established a high priority on spiritual matters in the hearts of the children. Seeing the faithfulness of Jehovah-Jireh to provide the material things taught and reinforced valuable lessons to family members and servants alike.

Granted, we are not required to journey to a distant place of worship to offer extensive and expensive sacrifice offerings, and some may feel that the second tithe is not applicable to us today. However, a man's worship to God and his relationship with his family remain important and both are affected by work and money. It is still important that a man take time away from normal work in order to worship. Doing so affirms that he is acknowledging God in his life and he is trusting God to make up through His blessing what would have been earned while working.

> Tithing to the ministry is one of the principles of God's economic system, but it is not the only one, for there are many Christians who tithe and still struggle to make it financially.

What we now call holiday or vacation is an outgrowth of what began as holy days. Today, it is just as important for families to spend time together as it was then. To do so, money must be set aside for this purpose. Thus, it is still good financial practice to tithe to one's self. In this way, money to spend on family vacations and money to provide for family financial security is made available.

Many people, especially those in the ministry, share my experience of not being able to take vacations. For more years than I would like to admit, my wife and I and our four children did not go on a vacation together, apart from a few days to my parent's home, because we simply could not afford it. I assumed the reason we had so little money was simply due to the fact that I was a preacher. However, I now know that the real culprit was my ignorance of the fact that God has an econo bring me, and all of us, into God's prosperity.

While tithing to the ministry is one of the principles of God's economic system, it is certainly not the only one, *Social Security is not sufficient to meet all your needs.*

for there are many Christians who tithe and still struggle to make it financially. The principle of the second tithe is to break the yoke of financial bondage and bring the believer into financial prosperity.

Tithing to one's self before giving offerings

Tithing to one's self ought to take priority over the giving of offerings. I know some will find this difficult to accept, especially since we have been taught that one cannot out give God. I agree with that thinking, but insist that our financial priorities must be consistent with Biblical teaching, otherwise our giving is out of line and will not have the full blessing of the Lord upon it.

An individual ought not to give offerings until, first, he has tithed to support the ministry to which he is joined, and, second, he has tithed to himself so that he is able to provide

It is important to remember that the tithes were designed for our benefit!

for the welfare of his family. The family's welfare exceeds just the basic needs of food, clothes, and shelter. Though the mandatory paying of social security taxes is intended to provide some means of support upon retirement and may be argued by some as the second tithe, I would point out that this tax does not cover a family's emergencies or recreation. Therefore, I urge that at least a small percentage of one's income be set apart for these purposes.

Third tithe—for the poor

God has a deep and abiding love and concern for the poor. In the social laws God gave to Israel are numerous provisions for the care of the poor, widows, and orphans. The neglecting of these people always brought God's judgment upon the nation.

One of the unalterable characteristics of righteousness is providing for the needs of the poor and neglected. In Israel, the monetary provision for this ministry of caring came through a third tithe. Actually, it appears that this tithe for the Levites, aliens, orphans, and widows was collected at the end of every three-year period, which results in a third of a tithe each year (*Deuteronomy 14:28-29 and 26:11-15*).

In the present day, this obligation can be considered to be practically met through one of the following ways:

1. Personal gifts to the poor.
2. Through offerings given to the church, part of which is used to provide for the poor and needy within the church and the community.

3. By the paying of taxes, part of which is used by the various local, state, and national governments to provide for the poor and needy.

We ought to remember that there is a blessing upon the individual, the church, the community, or the nation that provides for the poor. Contrariwise, there is a curse.

Though these tithes reflect what God wants and expects from His creation, we must remember that they were designed for our benefit. "Bring all the tithes into the storehouse, that there may be food in My house, and prove Me now in this," says the Lord of hosts, "If I will not open for you the windows of heaven and pour out for you such a blessing that there will not be room enough to receive it" (Malachi 3: 10).

(F. Nolan Ball is an apostle to the body of Christ. In addition to being Senior Minister at The Rock of Panama City, Florida, he relates to and oversees the establishing of men and churches, both in the U.S. and other countries.)

Material adapted with permission from *God's Plan for Financing the Ministry*, by F. Nolan Ball (1992).

3

Five Fallacies about the Purposes of Money

Sometimes knowing what's wrong is just as important as knowing what's right.

by Os Hillman

A successful businessman once confided in another businessman who was known for his wisdom. "You know," he said, "I've made a lot of money and will soon be able to retire comfortably. I can do just about anything I want."

The wise man replied, "I've found that when businessmen think they've built a tree that is so tall it almost reaches Heaven, God often decides to shake the tree."

God loves you too much to let your money rule your life.

Trusting in riches

The minute we start trusting in riches, God shakes the tree to demonstrate who is the source of wealth and to turn us back to trusting Him completely. He did it in my life, and He'll do it in your life. The reason is that He loves us too much to allow us to continue down this self-dependent path.

All that I own, the talents I have, and the resources He allows me to have, are simply given to me for me to manage.

My father died when I was fourteen. His death had a devastating effect on our family finances. As a result, I developed a life message that said I would not allow myself to suffer financial need again. Over the years I worked hard to make this a reality. A stronghold developed on the subconscious level that led me to build financial security at the cost of those who were close to me. This even continued for twenty years after I became a Christian and attended church every week.

Finally, as a result of becoming aware of my problem and dealing with it, I reviewed the many fallacies that I had fallen prey to and incorporated a new understanding of finances in my own life. This led to freedom in the area of my view and use of money.

When Jesus came to earth, He came to do one thing: the will of the Father. Because of His love for the Father, obedience was foremost in His mind. Jesus, therefore, expects our obedience to be based out of our love for Him.

> *"Jesus replied, 'If anyone loves me, he will obey my teaching. My Father will love him, and we will come to him and make our home with him. He who does not love me will not obey my teaching. These words you hear are not my own; they belong to the Father who sent me."*
> (John 14:23-24)

So, when we find that we are not seeking to obey God in the principles He has given us, we realize we have a love problem. We really have not come to the place where we love God enough to obey His commands.

Following are five common financial fallacies we can fall prey to in our lives.

Fallacy #1—My money is to be used to buy anything I want

To this John replied, "A man can receive only what is given him from heaven." (John 3:27)

When I accept Christ into my life, I am saying to Him that He is now the Lord of my life. My life no longer is my own. What I own, the talents I have, and the resources He allows me to have, are simply given to me for me to manage. He isn't against us having more than our basic needs as long as we remain an instrument of His to use those resources for His purposes. Our primary goal is to make money to be used for His purposes. We are to be His bondservant, one who is a willing slave with no rights of his or her own.

Finances was one of the hardest areas for me to give up control over. Was I truly willing to have only what Jesus desires me to have materially? I am not saying that God cannot bless a Christian materially. The important factor is whether God gave us what we have, or whether we got it by striving to acquire more and more out of the wrong motives.

You might say, "How can I really know this?" The best way is to pray and examine your motives for why you are working and earning money. Discuss the idea with your spouse or pastor, and ask God. Next, get into an accountable relationship with a few other men who are also willing to submit their finances to the Lord. Ask them to confirm through prayer whether your finances are lining up with what they believe God wants for you in this area. If we truly want Jesus lord over everything, it must start with our pocketbook.

Fallacy #2—My money measures my success

> *Command those who are rich in this present world not to be arrogant nor to put their hope in wealth, which is so uncertain, but to put their hope in God, who richly provides us with everything for our enjoyment.* (1 Timothy 6:17)

God clearly says that He hates pride. He warns us, "Pride goes before destruction, and a haughty spirit before stumbling. It is better to be of a humble spirit with the lowly, than to divide the spoil with the proud" (Proverbs 16:18). As a business owner, I became proud in heart and expected others to perform at a certain level, and if they didn't, I felt it reflected poorly on me. This pride of life was often reflected in my bank balance. However, because it was all on a subconscious level, I didn't recognize it as a problem. Others may not easily see it either, which is why it is so easy to fall prey to this sin.

We are constantly bombarded with messages about the next investment, retirement years, return on investment, etc. Our society drives us to focus our attention on equating success with money. Jesus never equated success with money. In fact, God cautioned us against the dangers that money created and a belief that our power is what gave us wealth. (See Deuteronomy 8:11-20)

Fallacy #3—Money is my security

> *The wealth of the rich is their fortified city; they imagine it an unscalable wall.* (Proverbs 18:11)

So many of us fall into this trap. God told the people of Israel that His name, Jehovah-Jireh, meant provider. We often want to insure ourselves against God. I learned the lesson

Your bank balance does not reflect your level of success.

that He and He alone is the provider of every need that I will encounter on this earth, even the smallest, most insignificant need. When our primary goal is wealth and independence, we fall into a trap. We think it is "an unscalable wall" against calamity, but we only deceive ourselves. Nothing can protect us if God decides we have misplaced our faith and security.

Personally, I found this to be the most difficult to avoid falling into. It is natural for us to want to be secure. But when we try to gain that security out of fear, we affront the nature of God. We are saying to God, "I don't think you will care for me, so I am going to make sure I will be secure."

A stronghold of insecurity and fear can make us susceptible to trying to save and hoard because of fear of what the future may bring. Building a wall of financial security around us can be a sign that money is being

It's natural for us to want to be secure. But when we try to gain that security out of fear, we affront the nature of God.

viewed as our security rather than God. When we fall into this we can expect God to remove our money in order to return our dependence on Him. Not out of punishment, but out of love for us.

Fallacy #4—I can gain independence by having a lot of money

Your heart became proud on account of your beauty, and you corrupted your wisdom because of

25

*your splendor. So I threw you to the earth; I made
a spectacle of you before kings.* (Ezekiel 28:17)

Security and independence are similar in focus. An independent spirit says, "I can do this fine by myself without others." When we say that to God, we are divorcing ourselves from Him. This will often cause us to lose our love for God, who wants us to depend on Him so that He can show how faithful He really is. This builds our faith and trust in Him to meet future needs. "Trust in the Lord with all your heart, lean not on your own understanding. Acknowledge Him in all thy ways, and He shall direct thy paths" (Proverbs 3:5-6).

Fallacy #5—Money defines my purpose in life

*But whatever was to my profit I now consider loss for
the sake of Christ.*

*What is more, I consider everything a loss compared
to the surpassing greatness of knowing Christ Jesus my
Lord, for whose sake I have lost all things. I consider them
rubbish, that I may gain Christ.* (Philippians 3:7-8)

This was an easy trap for me. Although it was subtle, I fell into the belief that the more money I had, the more value I had. This is the message the world is constantly communicating to us through every form of media—talk shows, commercials, Hollywood, and even the Church at times. Paul said the purpose for his existence was: "that I may know Him, and the power of His resurrection and the fellowship of His sufferings, being conformed to His death, in order that I may attain to the resurrection from the dead" (Philippians 3:10), and "to know the love of Christ which surpasses knowledge, that you may be filled up to all the fullness of God" (Ephesians 3:19).

Money is not what defines who we are—knowing Christ and His love defines our being. We should not be known by how much we own, what we do or know, or what we accomplish. Rather, we should be known by who we are as men and women in Christ.

Five fallacies about money

#1 My money is to be used to buy anything I want
#2 My money measures my success
#3 Money is my security
#4 I can gain independence by having a lot of money
#5 Money defines my purpose in life

(Os Hillman has had a career in marketing and advertising. He has authored several books; including, Proven Strategies for Business Success, The Five Fallacies of the Purposes of Money and his latest, Marketplace Meditations. He is also a teacher and consultant to organizations, empowering people to fulfill their calling through their work.)

4

The Seven Laws of Increase

When spiritual laws are mirrored in nature, it's for a good reason.

by Michael Q. Pink

Have you ever found yourself in the place where you were believing one of God's promises of provision while standing in the midst of financial lack, and instead of getting out of your problems, you were only sinking deeper?

I've read Philippians 4:19, "But my God shall supply all your needs according to His riches in glory by Christ Jesus," and explained to God that while I believed this to be true, my current circumstances were inconsistent with what I was reading in His Word. I told Him that while I knew His Word was the truth, I wasn't lying either, and I needed to understand why my experience was inconsistent with what I believed His Word promised. What He showed me changed my life.

If God's Word is true, then why am I coming up short financially?

29

Growth rings of life

I understood that God had "riches in glory," and that the streets of Heaven were paved with gold. I also had no doubt about His ability to provide, or of the abundance He possessed, but what I wanted to know was how to get some of the riches into the temporal realm so I could deposit them in my bank account and pay some very real bills with them.

As I walked through a wooded section of our property, I came across a large, sturdy, cedar tree. As I stood there admiring its strength and beauty, I heard the Father ask, "Where did the tree get its wood from?" Strange question, but since I had no answer, I said nothing. He gently said to my heart, "When you learn where the tree gets its wood from, you will know how to get the riches in glory into tangible form."

After checking out a book on botany from the local library, I soon discovered that in a previous generation, scientists of the day had done the same experiment—to learn where trees got their wood from. They planted a five-pound sapling in twenty pounds of earth inside a five-gallon pot, then placed it in a controlled environment where it could receive light and water as needed. Some years later, they removed the young tree and it weighed in at one hundred pounds, while the earth inside the pot weighed just a fraction less than the original twenty pounds. This gain of ninety-five pounds of wood baffled the scientists and greatly intrigued me. I continued my search.

The promise of God we want for our lives may very well not be the same promise He has for us.

As I read, seven ingredients necessary to produce a tree began to emerge. A pattern of seven often indicates a hidden spiritual truth, so I investigated more closely, especially since Jesus used agricultural illustrations to communicate profound spiritual truths, such as in the parable of the sower. Using Scriptural parallels of the ingredients, I pieced together "The Seven Laws of Increase."

Law # 1—Good soil

The first element necessary to produce a tree is soil. Soil must be prepared to receive the seed, and Jesus compares the soil to our hearts; therefore, the first law of increase is, "Prepare your heart."

In the parable of the sower, Jesus describes four different heart conditions:

A. If you have a hard, ungrateful heart, you won't be able to receive the seed of God's Word in your heart. Your doubt and cynicism will allow no place for the hope of His promise.

B. If you have a shallow heart with stony places, you are easily offended and when things don't go the way you think they should, you abandon the hope of His promise.

C. If your heart is crowded with the weeds of the cares of this world, including the deceitfulness of riches and the lusts of other things, the seed that is planted in your heart will soon be choked out and rendered fruitless.

D. A heart that has been plowed up with all its rocks removed and its weeds destroyed, exposing the soft rich texture of a tender heart, is prime to receive the seed of God's Word and bring forth a harvest.

Law # 2—Seed

The second element necessary to produce a tree is of course the seed itself. Jesus compared His Word to a seed that the Sower sows in your heart. The second law of increase is, "Receive the dream—in seed form."

One common mistake is to choose the seed we want and plant it in our heart, instead of letting the Sower plant the seed He wants to plant. Many times, we pick the promise we want to see manifested in our lives, while perhaps all the while God may be wanting to bring correction, possibly in an area of covetousness. If you let God be the Sower in your life, the seed He plants will bring forth the crop you need in the season you need it.

Law # 3—Good nutrients

The third element necessary to produce a tree is a good supply of nutrients. Just as nutrients promote seed growth and toxins deter it, our attitudes and belief systems can support or hinder the effect of God's Word in our heart. What we believe about God's Word will significantly impact the result in our life, therefore the third law of increase is, "Renew your mind."

What you don't know CAN hurt you.

Get firmly established in what you believe about God, sin, destiny, His kingdom, grace, mercy, faith, hope, love, etc., by reading what He has recorded for us in His Word. For example, if you have no concept of the destiny God has for you, you may not receive a promise in His Word about your future. An understanding of sound doctrine on central issues is critical to promote the growth of God's promises for your life.

Law # 4—Good water

The fourth element to produce a tree is of utmost importance: water. The fourth law of increase is, "Soak in the Word."

In Scripture, water is a type of two things: the Word and the Spirit. Interestingly, water is two parts hydrogen and one part oxygen. Oxygen can be compared to the Spirit or breath of God, while the two parts Hydrogen can be compared to the two forms of God's Word, the *logos* (written word) and the *rhema* (spoken word). Just as natural water nourishes and strengthens the root system, the water of God's Word strengthens and nourishes our spiritual roots.

Seven laws of increase

1. Prepare your heart
2. Receive the dream in seed form
3. Renew your mind
4. Soak in the Word
5. Seek God for a revelation
6. Walk in love
7. Convert trial to triumph

When we spend time just satiating in God's Word, we find ourselves encouraged, strengthened, counseled, cleansed, reproved, corrected, established, confident, and convinced of the love, mercy, and grace of God. This strengthens the roots of the fresh seedlings of God's Word that He has just planted in our heart to guide us through a specific time of testing.

Law # 5—Sun light

The next critical element necessary to produce a tree is light. What is light but a revelation of God's will for you to guide you through life? He gives that revelation through His Word, which is a lamp to our feet and a light to our path. The fifth law of increase is, "Seek God for a revelation."

Just as light energy produces chemical energy in a plant, so a revelation from God produces faith energy in our life. When God reveals His will to us, the lights go on and faith is released. This faith needs a proper motivation to succeed.

Law # 6—Warmth

Plants must have warmth to grow. What is warmth if it isn't love? Scripture says "Faith worketh by love." In other words, cars work by combustible engines, lights work by electricity, but faith works by love. If faith isn't motivated by love, it's like trying to run a car on something other than the fuel it requires. Love in action is the result of true faith. Love lays down its life for the good of others. The sixth law of increase is, therefore, "Walk in love."

As we walk in love, serving others from the heart, our character is formed, and the other seeds God has planted in our hearts begin to grow, mature, and come to fruition. Where the love of God does not abound in our hearts, there is no warmth to nurture the seeds of God's Word and they lay dormant, never coming to harvest in our lives.

Law # 7—Good air

The seventh critical element necessary to produce a tree is air. A tree breathes carbon dioxide (CO_2), much of which is produced by "animal breath"—ours and the beast of the field. The tree then separate the carbon from the oxygen and releases the life-giving oxygen back into the air. Then it combines the carbon with hydrogen and oxygen it gets from water to produce C6H12O6, a simple sugar that is the food it needs to sustain itself and grow.

Every problem has its matching opportunity.

Life often gives us "animal breath" instead of pure oxygen. We need to separate the good from the bad, giving off life-giving oxygen to those around us while turning that nasty carbon dioxide into opportunity by combining it with the Word and Spirit of God's Word (hydrogen and oxygen—H_2O) to produce our sustenance. Law number seven, therefore, is "Convert trial to triumph."

Joshua and Caleb of old, looked at the giants in the land and seeing them as God's provision for Israel declared, "they are but bread for us!" They did not see a problem, they saw an opportunity.

Opportunities are guarded by problems. When life gives you animal breath, turn it into provision.

I once had a customer cancel an order for 5000 of my leather-bound books that I was having specially printed for him. Everything was at the press and this cancellation came at a time when my wife and I could ill afford it. We asked the Father to show us how this could turn out to be His provision. He gave us an idea to turn that printing into a much less expensive paperback edition of the same book.

The book went on to become the most successful release in our publishing history. Truly, what came to us as animal breath turned into God's bountiful provision for us and another trial was converted to triumph!

When you plant the Word of God in a receptive heart, cultivated with good attitudes, regularly soaking in the water of God's Word in an environment of warmth, and seize the opportunity in every adversity, seeds will become trees and dreams will become realities. That is where trees get their wood.

(Michael Q. Pink has written over a dozen books, including Selling Among Wolves - Without Joining the Pack!, The Bible Incorporated and Promises Worth Keeping. He is the creator of the "Selling Among Wolves— Without Joining the Pack!" sales coaching program, and regularly helps corporations grow the revenue side of their business using Biblical strategies.)

5

Passing along Generational Wealth

The secret to long-range success is to build wealth in each generation.

by Dennis Peacocke

Lasting wealth is multi-generational, and it's oriented toward the long run, not the short-run. Remember, God is "the God of Abraham, the God of Isaac, and the God of Jacob" (Matthew 22:32). That's the three-generation principle. As a general rule, whatever God builds endures at least three generations. And, as a rule, it takes at least three generations for a major character trait to be implanted, or replaced, in a family.

The curse of poverty is single-generational wealth.

Curse of desertion

My great-grandfather once cut a winter's worth of wood, stacked it up next to the barn and deserted the family for twenty-five years. When he came back, he gave a British gold sovereign to my grandmother, who passed it on to my dad, who finally gave it to me. I had the coin made into a ring because it means so much to me. It reminds me that the curse I saw operating through my great-grandfather also had its effect on my grandfather and my father.

The curse of desertion that brought such great harm to their families ends in my generation. I am determined to leave a lasting inheritance to my children's children, and the ring on my finger is my reminder. My prayer now is that God will permit me to build through my children and grandchildren, three generations of family stewardship that will contribute mightily to the growth of the Kingdom of the God of Abraham, of Isaac, and of Jacob.

Curse of poverty

The curse of poverty is single-generational wealth. It is selfishness versus heritage. It is consumption versus savings. Inheritance tax and anti-family practices produce poverty. I heard some time back that Japanese corporate executives had bought large blocks of land in the Amazon rain forest. Why? Not primarily for profit, but to save the environment for their children!

Whatever the actual long-range realities of this situation turn out to be, the intent of these executives was right, and when we learned of this it sent us into mourning. Why are the Japanese acting as stewards of God's creation instead of Christian businessmen and women?

How do you witness to a non-believer who loves his children like that? The Japanese look at us as a "Christian nation" and say, "Thanks, but no thanks. We're not interested in that; we've got more going than you do." We must change the perspective of our families, businesses,

> "The vast majority of America's fortunes are dissipated within two generations."
> —George Gilder

communities, and nations to long-range thinking. Saving and investment, not consumption and debt, must drive our economy.

Passing on skills of stewardship and character

Godly families pass on the skills of stewardship and character as the primary guarantee of success—they don't emphasize things or money. Any man who wants his successful business to remain successful for generations to come, and to stay in the hands of the family, must train up his children to take over that business. They must understand the spirit that brings success—a long-run vision, care for people and relationship building, and an overall understanding that they are stewards accountable to God for how they handle everything He gives them.

Without character, an inheritance is short-lived.

We have no idea how much we're going to leave our children. We hope that, if Christ tarries, God will allow us to leave them something. But do you want to know what we really care about? We don't care much about leaving them things. We care about leaving them character skills, because someone with character skills can acquire all the things he needs. But someone who has things without character skills can't even hold onto those things, much less acquire more.

More importantly, all the things we pass on, and all the things our children acquire because of their character skills, will be burned up in the fire. Only the character skills will pass through to eternity.

Money isn't wealth

Many think that you have to inherit riches to be wealthy. Wrong! According to George Gilder, "The vast majority of America's fortunes are dissipated within two generations." Why? "When the money is actually passed on, [much of it] ends up among large numbers of prodigal sons and daughters... The receipt of a legacy, it turns out, often erodes the qualities of entrepreneurship that are needed to perpetuate it" (George Gilder, *Wealth and Poverty* [New York: Bantam Books, 1981] pages 74, 76).

The mistake many rich people make is never to teach their children to be wealthy. So, when the children inherit the riches, they waste it, spending it foolishly or investing in fools' projects.

The mistake many rich people make is never to teach their children to be wealthy.

The pattern of Jesus' high priestly prayer is the key to avoiding that waste: first cultivate wise stewardship in ourselves, and then through example, precept, and practice, cultivate it in our children. No one can achieve godly, mature, character without being responsible for the wise and faithful stewardship of private property.

I believe God wants to raise up Christian dynasties, families who teach their children from one generation to the next and build a snowball of wealth to use for God's Kingdom. But that will only happen as God's people learn, by the disciplined practice of managing private property, to be good stewards.

Those who get rich quick rarely stay rich for long—they don't have the skills to manage their riches.

40

Gaining riches too quickly

Riches gained quickly are soon lost (Proverbs 20:21). Why? Because if you gain too many riches too quickly, you won't have the skills to manage them. That's why those who get rich quickly rarely stay rich for long.

Accumulating riches is not based on how fast you get it. It's based on the ability to manage what you get responsibly. That's why gambling and get-rich-quick schemes never do anybody any good in the long-run. That's also why all the quick money-raising ideas church leaders come up with to finance their ministries, and the lotteries that more and more states are using to shore up their finances, will never work in the long-run.

Remember when the Israelites took the Promised Land? Moses said, "And the Lord your God will clear away these nations before you little by little; you will not be able to put an end to them quickly, lest the wild beasts grow too numerous for you" (Deuteronomy 7:22). The principle is simple: Don't take more that you can manage.

Investing in relationships is the key to wealth since it promotes covenantal responses (self-government) rather than short-run consumption. Christ's last act before His death was arranging for the care of His family. What a wonderful example for all of us to follow!

(One of the most compelling orators of our day, Dennis Peacocke is the president of Strategic Christian Services, New Cambridge Institute, and the Fellowship of Christian Leaders. He is regarded as a biblical strategist on an international level. Dennis and his wife, Jan, reside in Santa Rosa, California. They have three adult children.)

Used with permission from Rebuild, 1995.

II
Beating the Odds

6

The Secret to Solving Financial Problems

From personal to corporate, learn how to get out of financial pitfalls—for good.

by Thomas R. Noon, CPA

Are you having trouble with your personal finances? Or perhaps your business is on the brink of a financial crisis? You are not alone.

The United States is in the midst of the longest period of financial prosperity ever, unemployment is at record lows and the stock market at record highs. Yet personal bankruptcies are also at record numbers, and small and large companies struggle to stay afloat.

Over time, you will control your financial destiny.

Forget about why this happens, you need to make sure it doesn't happen to you. After 25 years as a CPA, Chief Financial Officer, and financial counselor, my cumulative and concentrated wisdom to solving financial woes is this: *create no new problems*.

Create no new problems.

I know, you are probably scratching your head and saying something like, "He doesn't understand what I'm in the middle of!" or "That is too simple!" or "How can I do that?"

Believe me! I have seen this simple principle guide people and companies out of terrible financial difficulties. I have used it myself to help our management team survive financial crisis long enough to turn the company around.

Remember, this works for either you personally or for your business! Financial problems are usually made up of many smaller problems that eventually add up to one big problem.

Diagram 1

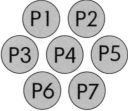

Financial problem
(made up of many small
financial problems)

Financial problems accumulate over time. Quite simply, they are based in the decision-making process of where you spend your income. Though most of us have complete control over these decisions, it seems that the critical and

The concentrated secret to financial success: create no new problems.

Diagram 2: The wrong way

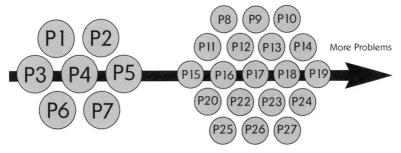

urgent problems (the proverbial "squeaky wheel") get addressed first. The individual/business who is yelling at you the loudest or has the biggest sword hanging over your head will naturally get your attention first.

These financial problems are usually based on owing money to others. The longer a debt is outstanding, the more intense the problem becomes, and the collection procedures become harder and harder to deal with. To solve such a financial problem, we normally try by putting our attention on and responding to the most intense collection procedure or urgent situation at the time. This is definitely the WRONG APPROACH!

You did not get into trouble by having good habits, so you won't get out of the crisis without change.

You may solve one individual problem, but a new one is almost always created to take its place. Over time, your total problem gets out of hand. This wrong approach is like a snowball rolling down a hill. Something needs to be done to level out the slope—but what?

The right approach

The right approach to financial problem solving is to draw a line in the sand and say, "After today, no new problems!"

It is all a matter of where you focus your attention. Trying to solve individual pieces to a whole problem will keep the snowball rolling down the hill as it constantly picks up new problems. The only way to level the playing field is to pay attention to the strategies that keep you from creating new problems.

In the financial arena, the line you draw is when you develop a "zero based budget" (ZBB). The ZBB comes to a break-even bottom line, which means you are creating no new debt. Over time, you will control your financial destiny. Since all your debt repayment is a part of your ZBB, your debts get paid over time and you eventually break into the fresh air of financial independence.

But be aware that you will be forced to make choices, some of them rather difficult. In your business, you may need to cut your overhead or find financing for that new marketing program to increase your income. Personally, you may be forced to cut the money spent on clothing, entertainment, or eating out. You may need a part-time job for a while to increase your income.

You did not get into trouble by having good habits, so you won't get out of the crisis without changing something.

The only way to solve a financial problem is to grab the reins of the wagon you're on, which is headed over a cliff, and

Diagram 3: The right way

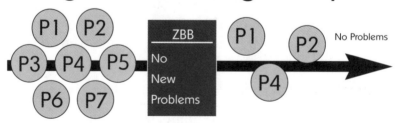

say, "I am going to control where this wagon is going. I am going to gain control over my expenses and make them less than my income."

Personal financial problem or company financial problem, the answer is the same! So, if you are tired of living on the slippery slope of ever-increasing pressures caused by your finances, change where you focus your attention. Don't let the squeaky wheel get the oil! Base all your financial decisions on a budget that you have created—and stick to it!

It may take some time, but the day will eventually come when your finances are problem-free.

The day will eventually come when your finances are problem-free!

(Thomas Noon is an executive with twenty-five years of financial management and public accounting experience. As a Chief Financial Officer, Tom improved bottom line results and built business value in a wide array of industries, including Internet communities, electronic commerce, publishing, retailing, media, software development, and venture capital.)

7

How to Get Out of Debt

**Being debt-free is not only an attainable goal,
it's an incredible lifestyle.**

by Patrick Morley

A debt-free pastor wrote this to me:

> Over seventy percent of my men are in farming
> and ranching. If I say something to them about my
> view of debt, their response is, "Yeah, but you were
> never in farming. You can't make it in this business
> without large loans and taking on debt."

> Three of my men are entering a home
> construction venture. "Looks real promising," they say.
> But it involves big loans from the bank.

> Some of my men are under almost unbelievable
> stress. Hail, drought, and harsh weather have made
> this year especially disappointing.

> One of my best men was advised by his lawyer a
> year ago to declare bankruptcy, which he didn't do.
> "I'm looking to lose $50,000 this year," he told me last
> Sunday. He is really under pressure, and is
> working his tail off. He scarcely has time for his
> precious wife and two teenage children.

> What is your counsel to these kinds of Christian
> men? Can one make it in business, construction,

farming, or ranching today without all this risk, pressure, and large debt?

What advice would *you* give this pastor?

The Problem of Debt

In December of 1995, a record 18.8% of after-tax income went to repay consumer installment debt (add in auto leases and home equity loans and the ratio increases to an unprecedented 21.6%).

In my opinion, the second biggest practical problem facing men today is debt pressure. (Number one? Over 40% of Christian marriages end in divorce). No pressure gets a man down like debt. The pressure to repay debt can feel like the powerful tentacles of a giant sea monster pulling you down into the suffocating deep.

> Debt is nothing more than borrowing from future income to buy what we cannot afford with current income.

Debt is nothing more than borrowing from future income to buy what we cannot afford with current income. Some debt, like a manageable-sized home mortgage, may make good sense. Most debt, however, does not.

Like a silky-voiced siren, our culture seduces men into the bondage of debt. We buy things we don't need with money we don't have to impress people we don't like. As said in *Wall Street: The Movie*, "The problem with money is that it makes you do things you don't want to do."

Here is a great truth:

> If you are not content where you are, you will not be content where you want to go.

The only problem with borrowing money is that you have to pay it back. Why doesn't it occur to many otherwise intelligent men that it takes more energy to earn a living and service debt than it takes to just earn a living?

What does the Bible say?

The Bible offers no prohibition against debt, but certainly doesn't encourage it. The Bible is full of cautions against debt and offers much counsel about how to overcome the negative consequences. Further, debt is never recommended.

When any issue we face has no specific command in the Bible, our duty is to be wise. Here are just a handful of scriptures that offer us wise counsel.

The rich rule over the poor, and the borrower is servant to the lender (Proverbs 22:7).

Men are under almost unbelievable stress.

He who puts up security for another will surely suffer, but whoever refuses to strike hands in pledge is safe (Proverbs 11:5).

Let no debt remain outstanding, except the continuing debt to love one another (Romans 13:8).

Do not be a man who strikes hands in pledge or puts up security for debts; if you lack the means to pay, your very bed will be snatched from under you (Proverbs 22:26-27).

Personally, I winked at these last verses (Proverbs 22:26-27), which caused me to go off the deep end.

When the Tax Reform Act of 1986 was passed, all capital stopped flowing into leveraged real estate. I found myself with a mountain of personally guaranteed mortgages, no permanent financing in sight, a dried up equity market, an over-built market place, and no way out. I had ignored the wisdom of Proverbs and made a real snarl of my business life. It took me seven years to get into debt. Little did I know that it would also take me seven agonizing years to get out.

"If Americans understood that their chances of winning a big lottery jackpot were 10 to 20 million to one, but that they could accumulate hundreds of thousands of dollars through regular saving, more families would put $50 away rather than spend it on gambling or unneeded consumption."

Joseph Plumeri, Primerica Chairman

Attitude: How you can get out of debt

Getting out of debt is an attitude before it is an action. To get out of debt one must despise the debt he has. He must sense a compelling need to get out of debt bondage, live by the wisdom of the Scriptures, and be set free.

It is the authority of the Scriptures and not our own experience upon which we must rely. True, it may *appear* in our experience that there is no way to get by without debt. But is that true? I think not. Too many debt-free people testify otherwise. We must interpret our experience by our Bible, not interpret our Bible by our experience. Only the Bible gives us a reliable guide for all matters of faith and life.

Action: What to do?

In January of 1987, I was reading along in Proverbs and saw the following verses in a way they have never struck me before—they got personal.

My son, if you have put up security for your neighbor, if you have struck hands in pledge for another, if you have been trapped by what you said, ensnared by the words of your mouth, then do this, my son, to free yourself, since you have fallen into your neighbor's hands: Go and humble yourself, press your plea with your neighbor! Allow no sleep to your eyes, no slumber to your eyelids. Free yourself, like a gazelle from the hand of the hunter, like a bird from the snare of the fowler. (Proverbs 6:1-5).

The only problem with borrowing money is that you have to pay it back.

From the moment these verses connected with me existentially—where I lived, I made it the ruling goal of my life *to get completely out of debt.* I applied the Proverbs 6 principle. After seven painful years, I can say that today I own no man anything except the continuing debt of love.

To be debt-free releases enormous creativity and energy. No longer am I consumed with plotting and scraping to make debt payments. No longer am I unable to get back to sleep at 2:00 a.m. No longer do I feel the stress in my marriage. No longer do I feel like some sea monster is dragging me under. I have caught my breath. Indeed, it does take less energy to earn a living than to earn a living and service debt.

Getting out of debt is a long-term project. It requires a willing heart, a concrete plan, and a disciplined approach.

It is never impossible to get out of debt.

But it can be done. In fact, it is being done by thousands of men, women, and couples right now.

To learn more about good stewardship, take a Crown Ministries course if available in your city (407-331-6000), contact Larry Burkett's organization (Christian Financial Concepts, (770-534-1000), or read *Master Your Money* by Ron Blue. Consider contacting a fee-based financial planner with similar values to help you construct a concrete debt-elimination plan.

Do it now! "Go and humble yourself; press your plea with your neighbor! Allow no sleep to your eyes, no slumber to your eyelids. Free yourself."

Six practical ideas: Do you need capital?

Here are six common sense ideas if you must have capital beyond your immediate cash resources:

#1. Accept only non-recourse financing. In other words, there is no personal liability beyond the financed asset. If the project fails, the lender can only look to the financed asset as collateral, not your very bed.

#2. Settle for less investment by going unleveraged. In other words, instead of investing $50,000 with half of it borrowed, settle for $25,000 worth of investment.

#3. Starting a business? Find equity partners and give up part of the ownership.

#4. Know your comfort zone. If you must borrow, don't borrow so much that you end up in a pressure zone.

#5. Limit any borrowing to a home mortgage and possibly a car payment. But drive the car twice as long as usual and escrow money each month so you can buy the next one for cash.

#6. Pay extra money each month on your mortgage (it all goes to principal reduction), even if it's only $50 or $100. If you can, make double payments to pay off your home early. Remember, in one sense, you are renting your financed home from your lender, you don't own it until it's fully paid off.

Applications

How about you? Are you under a load of debt pressure? Do you think it's healthy to go on that way? What could possibly be your motivation to be in debt beyond wanting to keep up the lifestyle you have, or increasing your lifestyle? Is this safe? Is this wise?

Here is the acid test: Because of your debt, if you suddenly died or became disabled, would your wife and children be able to continue their current lifestyle? Or, would they be forced to abandon it because you spent money, that should be going to life and disability insurance, to make debt payments on a lifestyle higher than you could really afford?

Getting out of debt requires a willing heart, a concrete plan, and a disciplined approach.

What's your next step? Will you take it?

(Pat Morley is a best-selling author, sought after speaker, and successful businessman. CEO and Founder of Man in the Mirror, Patrick is also the Chairman of the National Coalition of Men's Ministries. His most recent book is Second Wind for the Second Half, published by Zondervan.)

8

How to Get Yourself Rehired

Ten practical steps to finding a new—and better—life.

by Denny Brown

It seems like a normal day as you enter your office, remove your coat, and settle in to work. However, you notice that it does seem a bit quiet. Thinking nothing of that, you start retrieving voicemails and getting your day started. Suddenly, your boss enters with his administrative assistant. They close the door and sit down in solemn fashion.

"This is very difficult," is the opening remark. All of a sudden you get that sinking feeling that you are about to become very involved in this process. "We are going to have to let you go," he says bluntly.

There is no better time than the present to start!

Three questions inevitably come to your mind. How could I be so dumb as not to know? How am I going to go on with no income? And where do I go from here? Suddenly faced with a whole new set of issues concerning mortgage payments, college tuition, orthodontia, and that new car you just signed for, you find that your security has been completely eliminated in an instant.

Devastation of sudden unemployment

Over the years I have not only been a victim of this occurrence, but I have regretfully had to cause this to occur in other people's lives. I have talked with many people who have gone through this unfortunate experience. For an employee who works hard, obeys the rules, and earns his pay, this can be truly a devastating experience.

What fascinates me, however, is that while some go into depression of various degrees, others not only go through the process, they survive it in victorious fashion. How do they do it? Admittedly, it is very difficult, but they have chosen to focus not on the negative but on the positive, recognizing that a fresh start could bring more benefit and excitement than previously imagined. I must admit, however, that the greatest secret to surviving these difficult times is a personal relationship with Jesus Christ.

Now here are ten practical steps to getting yourself rehired; and more importantly, your life back in order.

1. Get over the shock

It is certainly normal to feel sad and depressed over this turn of events. The question, however, is for how long and with whom? My suggestion is to get it out of your system quickly. If you must vent to others, a good suggestion is to limit yourself to two people, or two days, whichever comes first. Spare those who love you most, after all, they spend most of their non-working hours with you. Seek out a Pastor, or a close friend, who is willing and able to help.

How am I going to go on with no income?

This is also a good time to pray. God says, "You have not because you ask not," which is just one of His many promises of provision for you and for your family through these difficult times. Consider praying for those who may have previously hurt you and ask

God for the strength to forgive and to help you to move on with your life. Your first victory on the road back to employment can and will come through Him, just in knowing that He will protect and provide, sometimes in the most miraculous ways!

2. Take time for self-assessment

Next, determine to perform the self-assessment necessary for you to formulate and target your job search. Determine the best markets (jobs, industries) for you. Define your skills, competencies and experience; and define these in writing your resume and preparing yourself for the eventuality of an interview.

Much material has been written that will assist you in preparing for, organizing, and executing your job search. A visit to job networking sites on the Internet, or a visit to the library or your local bookstore, will be of great help.

Attend those seminars that you would not normally have time to attend and read trade journals that have been stacking up.

Take several days and rethink about your practical skills. Ask yourself what you would do vocationally for the rest of your life. Your whole focus is planning for the future. Visit with and ask family and friends. Review your abilities with former co-workers. They may have good input for your consideration.

This is a good opportunity to pray for God's direction asking Him to open up new opportunities for you to pursue. There may be a whole new endeavor out there for you to experience. Pray, asking God what is really important to you and your family. Jesus said, "I am come that you might have life, and have it more abundantly." Consider for a moment the word abundance, what the Lord meant by using it, and how that can be applied to your life both now and in the future.

3. Find a job-hunting system that will work for you

While there are countless great books and software programs on the market, the key is getting a system that works for you. You want to be proactive and calm, not filled with fear and desperation. Attend the meetings in your town for job seekers that will provide you with knowledge you may need. Just as importantly, become involved in community service organizations, chambers of commerce, and other arenas where you will be exposed to and involved with employed people who can help. As you take each action step, ask yourself, "Will this move me one step closer to my objective?"

Ask God to open doors for you and to give you the confidence necessary to enter into a situation of unknowns and to succeed. Perhaps the most difficult thing in the world is to enter a new organization and strive to make new friends and networking opportunities in a very short time frame. For most of us, it is a step in faith as well as an opportunity to observe, on a firsthand basis, the ability of God to do a miraculous work!

4. Take care of you

This is a time to get plenty of sleep, exercise and eat nutritious stress-fighting food. It's best to follow a routine that is good for your body and spirit. I also recommend that you maintain your normal work schedule. Get up and get dressed and go to work. Your present employment just happens to be the business of job hunting. If necessary, get out of the house. Perhaps someone you know would let you use office space. This self-discipline will pay off in the long run.

Get over it! If you must vent to others, limit yourself to two people, or two days, whichever comes first.

Taking good care of yourself will increase your energy and put you in a better position for your interviews. When you are speaking on the phone, people are only hearing your

Remain proactive and calm, not filled with fear and desperation.

voice without the aid of an energetic you, so you want to come across with a zest for life that conveys the image you want to project. At the same time, take some time off on a regular basis, just as you would if you are working. Time for your family and time for yourself is just as important as it ever was!

5. Learn to network

Let people know what you are looking for in a job. If they hear of something that would be a fit for your background, they need to think of you, and they need good information in order to make those connections. Frequent communication using a thirty-second resume really helps.

Expand your circle of acquaintances. This is not the time to be shy and withdraw. Attend professional meetings, trade shows, and anywhere you will come in contact with those who make hiring decisions for your field and/or your peers. Help other business people make human connections that may help them in business or lead them to a new opportunity. People remember who helped them reach their objectives and goals.

Rarely do job seekers think that by helping others they are actually helping themselves. For example, by helping recruiters with candidate leads, you will often accrue a benefit for yourself in that you will be on their minds, not only as a candidate, but also as a pretty good person! This, and other acts of service, will go a long way and are hard to forget.

6. Develop your job leads

Internet, Internet, Internet—this is the time to take advantage of the many opportunities that are on the Web. From job boards that will e-mail you when a match is found to corporate web sites with current job postings—there is a wealth of good assistance available at no cost to you. It is estimated that there are about 20,000 job sites on the Internet ranging from general to specialized jobs.

Get up and get dressed and go to work. Your present employment just happens to be the business of job hunting.

People, People, People—see more, touch more, and make sure they know about you. It is a fact that very few jobs are landed as a result of just answering an ad and getting hired. As you go up the ladder in terms of salary, you are becoming more dependent upon the people you know and their recommendations of you. It is imperative to reach out to people and let them get to know you and your talents.

And, very importantly, keep your attitude positive.

7. Accept help

People want to help and are usually willing to help you if you just ask. The American business system is based upon business people doing favors for one another. Sometimes our independent work nature gets in the way of asking others to assist us. Just try it and see what results you receive.

Remember, it's okay to accept some help. You, too, will be there for them in whatever ways you can be.

8. Keep your attitude and spirit positive

Focus on the outcome and enjoy the journey. When you think about how long you have worked in your life, this is really a brief time. And even though it has its own set of stresses, look for ways to build components into the search to make it a special time. You may not be in this position of having some extra time for a long time. Other than work, what really gives you joy? Enjoy as much as you can along the way.

Also, get rid of the guilt and shame that can arise from unemployment. There is not one person with whom you will come in contact with who does not have the potential of becoming unemployed in an instant. They just haven't decided that it could ever happen to them. The best way to get rid of the guilt and shame is to give it to God in prayer and let Him strengthen you. Also, foster the friendships you build with those who know and appreciate from first-hand experience the difficulty of not working.

9. Accept your new job

The ten steps to finding a new and better job

1. Get over the shock
2. Take time for self-assessment
3. Find a job-hunting system that will work for you
4. Take care of you
5. Learn to network
6. Develop your job leads
7. Accept help
8. Keep your attitude and spirit positive
9. Accept your new job
10. Keep yourself ready

When the day finally comes and all your efforts have paid off with a new job, please remember to thank those who helped you and resolve to reach out to others you met along the way. You have had new experiences in your job search that could very well help someone else. Always watch for these opportunities and seize them.

There is not one person you will come in contact with who does not have the potential of becoming unemployed instantly.

10. Keep yourself ready

We all know that circumstances change. Businesses merge, companies make changes very quickly, and start-ups sometimes stop. Stay ready, keep your networks alive and help others do the same. At least to some degree, we should all stay in the job market, since the only constant today is God Himself.

And when it's all said and done, keep in mind Who brought you through.

(Denny Brown is co-leader of JobSeekers in Atlanta, a Business Development Specialist and a coach to CEOs. He has thirty years of corporate experience as Chairman of the Board, President/CEO, Business Owner, National Sales Manager and other positions. He and his wife, Sharon, live in Atlanta and have two children and two grandchildren.)

III

Personal Money Management

9

Budgeting Your Money

After all, it's YOUR money you're saving.

by Charles Ross

Before you embark on a budgeting program, determine your goals, whether they include increasing savings, reducing debt, or getting more for your buck out of your insurance programs.

Next, find out your monthly net income or take-home pay. This is the amount of money you actually receive from your employer after your tithes, taxes, and other deductions are taken out.

Adding up your total monthly expenses is the next step. Gather up your receipts, look through your canceled checks, and try to see exactly where your money went last month. Write these figures down and separate them into categories: housing, food, automobiles, and so on. The general budget categories and percentages below are to help you in the design of your own budget.

Taxes (variable percent)

If you have ever thought about not paying your taxes, or better still, fudging a little, consider again. The Bible says, "Give everyone what you owe him: If you owe taxes, pay taxes; if revenue, then revenue; if respect, then respect; if honor, then honor" (Romans 13:7). We are to pay our taxes, and in return we expect a system that works for the well-being of the whole society.

When looking at this item in your budget, make sure you are not overpaying taxes. Many people maintain that the only way they can save money is to overpay their taxes and get a refund. This is not good stewardship. You may need that extra money throughout the year to take care of other family expenses. In essence, you are loaning your money to the government but receiving no interest on it.

If you don't know how many exemptions you need to claim to have the correct amount taken from your paycheck, here is what you can do. Look at last year's tax return and make sure you pay at least 100 percent of the total amount of taxes that you owed for that year. Divide that amount by the number of pay periods in the year, then instruct your employer to deduct that amount from your paycheck. For example, if your total federal tax bill came to $5,000 and you get paid twice a month, you would have your employer deduct $208.33 every pay period ($5,000 divided by twenty-four).

Housing (30 percent)

I realize that 30 percent is a very low number, given the fact that it includes other items, but I will always be conservative about expenses. Many people stretch themselves to buy a house, but your home should *never* cost more than 38 percent of your net income. This amount includes your mortgage payment, taxes, insurance, and utilities. If your budget goes over in one category, you have to compensate in another. You may be able to spend 40 percent of your net income on housing, but perhaps you don't have a car payment to make. It all has to balance out.

Consider these other spending tips.

- Try to get on the budget plan for electricity and gas. You want to try to fix your expense items in your budget so that you can predict the payment.

- Take all the proper discounts for home owner's or renter's insurance.

- Don't forget that you will have to maintain your home, so factor that cost into the budget. This amount may average 5 to 10 percent of your total monthly mortgage payments.

Food (12 percent)

Overspending on food is easy to do. With the increasing pressure on supermarket chains to be profitable, they have devised layouts to increase the time you spend in the store because they know that the more time you spend in the store, the more money you will spend.

Before you budget, decide on your goals.

Reducing or just controlling your spending in this category will require planning. Of course, one of the best ways to limit spending is to plan your meals in advance. If you do this, you will shop only for items to complete the menus, and you will make better use of your time and money. These other tips may be useful.

- Always shop with a written list.

- Never go shopping when you are hungry.

- Take a calculator along, and add up items as you shop to stay on budget.

- Shop at one of the warehouse stores (such as Sam's).

- Check out advertised specials.

- Use coupons, but use them only for items you would normally buy.

- When possible, purchase groceries in bulk quantities (cups, napkins, paper plates, etc.).

- Do not take your children with you. Studies show that parents tend to spend more money when children tag along.
- Make sure that the cashier rings up the items correctly.
- Compare prices of store brands to prices of national name brands.

Car maintenance (variable percent)

Unless you are able to work on your car, I believe the best way to save on car maintenance costs is to find an honest and reputable mechanic to do the work for you. If you are not able to do all the repairs, perhaps you can do the routine maintenance items, such as oil change, lubrication, and tune-ups. Most cars now come with a list of routine maintenance activities. You should follow the manufacturer's suggestions for maintenance.

Manuals such as *Mitchell's Parts and Labor Estimating Book*, which may be at your local library, will give you the estimated cost for parts and time per repairs. Compare several mechanic's prices before servicing your car. And always ask to keep the old parts.

How many exemptions do you claim? Divide last year's total taxes paid by 12, then have your employer deduct that amount per month.

Insurance (5 percent)

Families seem to overpay or underpay for insurance because they don't have a method for determining whether they have the proper coverage. Most people need several forms of insurance, including life, health, auto, home, and disability. Take time to sit down with your respective insurance provider to determine your needs and provisions.

Debts (5 percent)

Most families have a problem with debt because they generally are living a more expensive lifestyle than their budget will allow. They finance their lifestyle by using credit cards. The guideline budget can include a 5 percent debt level, but if you are spending 15 percent or more of your net income on debt payments, then you are in way over your head. You should stop using credit immediately and start living on cash.

Your home should never cost more than 38 percent of your net income.

Entertainment/Recreation (5 percent)

Who says you can't have fun on a budget? We need to learn to rest, relax, and take necessary breaks, but not in a way that drives us deeper into debt. If you finance your fun with debt, you will not be having fun for long.

When planning vacations, try to schedule them during the off-seasons so that you will not pay high prices. Ask the agent for the lowest possible airfare and some alternatives. Plan your trips far enough in advance so that you can shop for discounts. Instead of a long vacation, think about a three or four day stay, and spend the balance of your vacation at home. Discover low-cost or no-cost ways to relax in your hometown.

Savings (10 percent)

You have heard it before—pay yourself first. If you don't, borrowing will become a way of life. Many people get into credit trouble not because they use their credit cards to support a lavish lifestyle, but because they have no savings. When an emergency arises, then they are forced to tap that credit line to take care of it.

The best way to save is through payroll deductions. Your employer deducts a set amount from your paycheck and it is deposited into your saving account. If your employer does not provide this service, then ask your bank to draft your checking account a day or so after your paycheck is deposited and put it into a savings account.

Many people try to write a check to their savings account each month, but the money never seems to make it to the savings account. If you don't have the discipline to deposit money into your savings account and not touch it, then you will never, ever be financially independent.

Medical expenses (5 percent)

Place in your budget the amount of your deductible. You know that you will have to pay that before the insurance pays anything. If your deductible is $250 a year, spread that amount over twelve months, or $20 a month. Do not sacrifice your family's health due to lack of planning. Make sure that your family members go to the doctor for regular checkups and that you practice preventative medicine. Don't be afraid to get a second opinion, since doctors and hospitals vary with what they charge.

> A basic budget can include 5% toward debt reduction, but if you are spending 15%, you are in way over your head!

Miscellaneous (8 percent)

This category includes all the items that did not fit in the other categories. You might have to add additional ones that are unique to your situation, such as child support or alimony.

Concerning allowances, spouses need to feel that they have money they don't have to be accountable for, which means each spouse ought to get the same weekly allowance. They then have the freedom to spend a certain amount of money as he or she sees fit. The amount should be ample enough to take care of parking, lunches, tolls, or other regular weekly expenses.

Anything left?

Now, subtract your monthly expenses from your net income. Do you have anything left? Good! if not, you are spending more than you earn. You need to cut expenses or find ways to increase your income if you're going to stay in good financial health.

Implementing your budget.

Many people cash their paychecks, put a little in the checking account, and pocket the rest. To become a better money manager, try depositing all of your income into your checking account and paying your bills and expenses by check. This method will allow you to keep track of your income and expenses and will also make it easier later when you have to review your budget and make adjustments. If you have a computer, you can save a lot of time by using a money management program, like *Quicken* or *Microsoft Money*.

Another idea is to use an expense diary, which helps you track expenses, small and large, on a daily basis. A pocket-sized diary is easy to carry, and you can record expenses and store receipts in it. Maintaining your checkbook will support your expense diary records. Noting your expenses will be important for completing your

Subtract your monthly expenses from your net income. Do you have anything left?

budget and doing your taxes at tax time. Impulse buying can ruin the best budget plan. By depositing all of your income in a checking account, you keep the money out of your hands so that you can't spend it.

For a budget to run smooth, like a car, it will require regular maintenance. Set aside time each month to review your budget, maybe at the same time as you balance your checking account. Are you spending too much in any given area?

Pay yourself first. If you don't, borrowing will become a way of life.

Now that you finances are laid out, you may have to decide what to curtail or give up to reach your goals. Don't make it too painful. But if it doesn't hurt a little, you are probably not trying hard enough. Learn to live within your budget.

(Charles Ross is president of Financial Media Services, Inc., Christian Financial Ministries, and host and executive producer of the nationally syndicated radio program "Your Personal Finance." He is author of Your Common Sense Guide to Personal Financial Planning and God's Plan for Your Financial Success. He lives in Atlanta with his wife and three daughters.)

Adapted with permission from *God's Plan for Your Financial Success*, by Charles Ross. Published by Thomas Nelson Publishers, 1998.

Seven common money management mistakes

1. Having only one family member involved in the financial matters
2. Having no written goal
3. Having no budget
4. Having no money for emergencies
5. Having no tax planning
6. Not using employee benefits
7. Not spreading the risk of your investments

10

Maximize Your Estate for Values and Dollars

**Estate planning does not only apply
to the rich and famous.**

by Charles L. Stanley, CFP, ChFC

Estate Planning applies to just about everyone. It is generally true that the greater the wealth, the greater the significance of estate planning, but even single people with modest wealth should do at least minimal estate planning.

From a planning perspective, there are three different categories or levels—minimum, moderate, and advanced.

1. **Minimum Level** applies to anyone with minimal assets.

2. **Moderate Level** is for people who have enough assets to exceed their state's rules for an abbreviated probate (in California, for example, it is $100,000 for assets other than real estate or $10,000 for real estate. Since it is almost impossible to own real estate in California worth less than $10,000, the ownership of real estate alone qualifies one for this Moderate Level of Estate Planning.)

3. **Advanced Level** applies to anyone whose estate exceeds the allowable exclusion for Federal Estate Taxes. This is $675,000 per person in 2000 and will increase to $1,000,000 in 2006. (See the end of this chapter for a chart showing the increasing amounts year by year until 2006.) Be careful about this, however, without proper planning a spouse can easily lose their exemption.

Minimum Level Estate Planning

Every adult who owns any assets should have a properly drafted will. Simply, this will direct the disposition of those assets at the time of death. This is usually hard for younger adults to accept since they consider themselves immortal until about age 35 or so. For younger married couples with children, another critical element in a will is the nomination of guardians if Mom and Dad should die before the kids become adults. *Estate Planning applies to just about everyone.* The choice of the courts may be significantly different from yours without your guidance in your will.

In addition to a will, one should have two Power of Attorney documents created, one for healthcare and one for assets. The Healthcare Power of Attorney designates the person who you want to make healthcare decisions on your behalf should you be unable to do so (i.e. a coma victim due to accident or illness, or any time an individual is unable to make their will known in regard to their healthcare decisions). The person to whom the power is given should be someone who knows your beliefs and feelings about these kinds of issues.

The Power of Attorney for assets grants the person you name as attorney the authority to act like he/she owns the assets with one important exception: they are required to always act in your best interest and use the assets for your benefit. To do otherwise is a breach of fiduciary responsibility. Power of Attorney can take different forms— usually *Springing Power of Attorney* and *Durable Power of Attorney*. You will need to consult with your attorney as to which is correct for you.

- Springing Power of Attorney *springs* into action when you become disabled. It is of no use to the person named as attorney until your disability.

- Durable Power of Attorney is in force from the time it is signed and continues to be in force after a disability. (If a Power of Attorney is not *Durable*, it will be invalid upon your disability. For estate planning purposes, you will most certainly want a Durable Power of Attorney.)

The last document in this category is generally known as a Living Will. It is a document that states in writing your desires should you enter a persistent vegetative state (like a coma). Some people do not want any heroic efforts taken to keep them alive if they should ever be in this condition. Others want certain efforts taken and some not taken. Unless you put it down in writing and make copies available to your healthcare workers, they will not know what your desires are or be able to act upon them.

State law controls all of the documents mentioned above. It is important to have them drafted by an attorney who is admitted to practice in your state. If you frequent other states regularly, you should consider having documents drawn up for these states as well.

Beneficiary designations on company retirement plans such as a 401(k) plan, IRAs, annuities and life insurance should be reviewed periodically. Be sure the assets will go where you want when you do not need them anymore. As wealth grows, these designations can take on much greater significance because the estate plan takes on more complexity.

Every adult who owns any assets should have a will.

The best arrangement may not be obvious. Should you name a spouse or your family Trust (see below) as beneficiary of your annuity or life insurance? The correct answer is, "It depends." This complicated questions should be discussed thoroughly with your estate planner. Personal mistakes could thwart your good intentions.

Moderate Level Estate Planning

When a person acquires real estate, they have probably entered the Moderate Level. It could happen sooner, but it surely has by the time real estate is purchased. The benchmark is when your asset value has exceeded your state's statutory amount for performing a simplified probate.

At this point, probate becomes an issue. In some states probate costs are not excessive, but others, like California, can be onerous. Probate becomes something to avoid in most cases. Probate is simply the process of proving the validity of a will and arranging for the re-titling of assets to the new owner after the death of the previous owner.

The criticisms of probate are cost, time, and public exposure. Costs can run about 4% to 10% of the fair market value of the probate estate, and probate can take a few months or many years. Obviously, the longer it takes the more it costs. Finally, the will becomes public information. For some people this is extremely unnerving. How can this be avoided? The most highly promoted method is to create a Revocable Living Trust. For many people, having such a trust is a valuable technique.

Creating a trust

Creating a Trust is like creating a company. When it is formed, you put your assets in the Trust. You are the Trustee (the boss), the Beneficiary (the one who gets all the income and other benefits from the Trust), and the Trustor (the one who created the Trust). As Trustor, you have the right to change the Trust and even revoke it (go out of business, to follow our metaphor of a company). If you revoke the Trust, all the assets go back to the person who put them there in the first place, which is you! This does not change anything concerning income taxation and it does not protect your assets from a lawsuit.

What does it accomplish? The primary reason for most people creating a Living Trust is to avoid probate. When you die, if you have put all your asset into your Trust, you do not own anything to go through probate—your Trust does! And, your Trust did not die! Voilà! No probate.

With that said, it is important that the Trust be drafted correctly and be funded correctly. Funding has to do with transferring title to all your assets to your Trust. Your attorney should help you with this process along with your Financial Planner or stockbroker. This is critical.

If you do not fund your Trust, you just wasted your time and money because it is of no value if not funded.

Social Capital is the money that you do not ultimately get to keep. But you can direct it to your favorite charities.

If you create a Trust, your wills will need to be updated to reflect the existence of the Trust. At this point, the will generally becomes a "pour over will," which simply means that it will make sure anything you forgot to fund into your Trust will be directed there by your will. Unfortunately, you could still have a probate if you did forget to fund your Trust properly, but the will makes sure the distribution of assets goes according to your wishes as outlined in your Trust.

You will also want to revisit your beneficiary designations on your annuities and life insurance to see if they should be changed now that there is a Trust. A competent Certified Financial Planner" licensee (CFP) or Chartered Financial Consultant (ChFC) should be able to help you with this. (See the definition of CFP at the end of this chapter.)

Advanced Level Estate Planning

Now we get into the area that can potentially be very complicated. Anyone whose estate exceeds the amount exempt from the Federal Estate Tax fits this category. The Revocable Living Trust, in the case of married couples, takes on an additional significance.

Generally, couples should have what is called an A/B Trust. The idea is to preserve the Unified Credit for the first spouse to decease.

To illustrate, let's assume a couple, Mr. and Mrs. Smith are worth $2,000,000. At the death of the first (most likely, Mr. Smith, according to statistics), if we do not have a "B" or Credit Shelter Trust, also called the Decedent's Trust, all the assets will go to Mrs. Smith. There will be no Estate Tax because all the assets will transfer under the Unlimited Marital Deduction.

Tip #1—Do not attempt to do Estate Planning on your own without professional assistance. Software for will preparation can be purchased for very little. You can prepare a valid will with it. However, without knowledge of estate planning and probate law in your State, you may have a document that will not fulfill your wishes. This is not a place to skimp.

Now, Mrs. Smith has an estate of $2,000,000. Mrs. Smith is so affected by the death of her husband that as soon as his estate is settled, Mrs. Smith dies, too. Now the Estate Tax Return (IRS Form 706) is completed. This all happens in the year 2000 and so Mrs. Smith has an Estate Tax Exemption of $675,000. The remaining $1,325,000 is subject to Estate Tax.

Now let's suppose Mr. and Mrs. Smith were still alive and had done additional Estate Planning with an A/B Living Trust. In the event that Mr. Smith dies, Mrs. Smith would have received $1,325,000, as compared to $2,000,000, with Mr. Smith's exempt amount, $675,000, going into the "B" Trust.

A primary reason for most people creating a Living Trust is to avoid probate.

The important thing is that her $1,325,000, under the Unlimited Marital Deduction, has no Estate Tax attached to it. From the "B" Trust, Mrs. Smith receives all the income and can access the principal for needs: defined as health, education, maintenance, and support. Mrs. Smith has not given up access to the assets in the "B" Trust if she ever needs them.

If Mrs. Smith dies, now she has an estate of $1,325,000 (instead of $2,000,000) and her exemption of $675,000. The only amount subject to Estate Tax is $650,000 ($1,325,000 minus the $675,000 exemption), which is less than half the amount that would have been subject to the tax without the "B" Trust.

Since the "B" Trust was funded with the exempt amount, it passes Estate Tax free, regardless of how large it may grow. It may be subject to Capital Gains Tax, but never Estate Tax.

As you can see, with this mechanism of the A/B Trust, we can preserve the exemption for both Mr. & Mrs. Smith. However, we still have the $650,000 subject to tax.

Anyone whose estate exceeds the amount exempt from the Federal Estate Tax fits this category.

There are many techniques for dealing with our illustration type of excess that is subject to Federal Estate Tax. Of course, the particular circumstance of the family will dictate which technique may be appropriate. This is why it is critical that families consult with experienced Estate Planners who understand the client as a unique family and not simply as another prospect. You need to make your values known, since they should control the decision.

Irrevocable Trust

If you are happy to allow the Estate Tax dollars to go to the Federal Budget, but would like for your children's inheritance to be maximized, the most simple technique is to establish an Irrevocable Trust with the children being the beneficiaries. You make annual gifts to your children through the trust.

The trust buys a second-to-die or survivorship life insurance policy on your lives in an amount sufficient to cover the Estate Taxes. Since this is an irrevocable trust (I will assume it is properly drafted and funded, etc.), it is outside of your estate and will therefore pass totally tax free to your children.

If your anticipated Estate Tax bill was $375,000, for example, the trust would purchase a life insurance policy with a death benefit of at least $375,000. After both of you pass away, your children would have a tax bill for $375,000

Tip #2—Do use a professional who will first take time to get to know you and your personal values. This should help you to obtain a more satisfying plan.

and tax free cash in the amount of $375,000 with which to pay the taxes. This allows the children to have a full inheritance not reduced by the Estate Tax.

If, on the other hand, you would rather control the disposition of those dollars currently destined for the Federal Budget, and direct them instead to the charitable institution of your choice, there is another exciting step you can take. There are many techniques to do this, also.

Charitable Remainder Unitrust

One technique is to create a Charitable Remainder Unitrust and name your favorite charity or charities as the remainder beneficiaries (the ones who get what is left after your deaths). This type of trust, known as a split-interest trust (both you and the charities have an interest in it), allows you to have an income for either the rest of your lives or a term of years not to exceed twenty years.

When you fund the trust (make your gift), you get a charitable income tax deduction that is generally quite substantial. You have the year of the gift plus five more years in which to use the entire deduction. This method gives the biggest bang for the buck among the techniques mentioned here. You generally get a greater income than before the gift, and you get a charitable income tax deduction, your favorite charity gets a substantial gift after your death, and the IRS gets nothing. Assuming you have also created the irrevocable trust with life insurance mentioned above, your children get their full inheritance.

Social Capital

This is a very exciting opportunity for people with strong feelings against paying more taxes than necessary, and a heart to do good for others. You get to control what is generally referred to as your Social Capital. Social Capital is the money you do not ultimately get to keep.

Tip #3—For the upper end of the Moderate Level and the Advanced Level, hire a team of advisors to include a Certified Financial Planner licensee or Chartered Financial Consultant, an Estate Planning Attorney, and possibly a CPA.

But as you have seen, you can control it and direct it to your favorite charities like your church, mission organization, hospital, seminary or other educational institution. Any qualified 501(c)(3) organization can be the beneficiary on this type of plan.

Once you have taken the time to clarify your values as they relate to your Estate Plan, you can stay in control of the process and be sure it is accomplishing what you want for your estate.

You generally get a greater income than before the gift & your favorite charity gets a substantial gift after your death, and the IRS gets nothing.

Gift and Estate Tax Unified Credit and Exclusion Equivalent

Year Unified Credit	Exemption	Equivalent
2000-2001	$675,000	$220,550
2002-2003	$700,000	$229,800
2004	$850,000	$287,300
2005	$950,000	$326,300
2006	$1,000,000	$345,800

(IRC Sec. 2010)

(Charles L. Stanley is a Certified Financial Planner and a Chartered Financial Consultant. Financial Planning is his second career following twenty years as an ordained minister. His practice is concentrated in the areas of Estate Planning and Wealth Management, with a special interest in helping clients control their Social Capital.)

"CFP" and "Certified Financial Planner" are federally registered service marks of the Certified Financial Planner Board of Standards, Inc. ("CFP Board") The CFP Board licenses individuals who satisfy its educational, examination, ethics and experience requirements but does not warrant the correctness of advice given by such licensees, or the appropriateness of products or services recommended.

11

Money Management for Your Kids

Imagine knowing what you now know about finances—when you were twelve!

by Howard Dayton

Learning to handle money should be part of a child's education. Parents must direct this themselves and not delegate it to teachers because spending experiences are found outside the classroom. Consider five areas where this is possible.

1. Income

As soon as the child is ready for school, he should begin to receive an income to manage. The parents need to decide whether they wish to give an allowance or require their child to earn the income. Choose the alternative with which you are most comfortable.

The amount of the income will vary according to such factors as the child's age

The amount of the income will vary according to such factors as the child's age and ability to earn. However, the amount is not as important as the responsibility of handling money.

Five areas of training

1. Income
2. Budgeting
3. Giving
4. Saving and investing
5. Debt

and ability to earn. However, the amount is not as important as the responsibility of handling money. At first it is a new experience, and the child will make many mistakes. Don't hesitate to let the *law of natural consequences* run its course. You're going to be tempted to help little Johnny when he spends all his income the first day on an unwise purchase. You won't like the fact that he has to live the rest of the week without all the other things he wants and maybe needs. Don't bail him out! His mistakes will be the best teacher.

2. Budgeting

When children begin to receive an income, teach them how to budget. Begin with a simple system consisting of three boxes, each labeled by category—give, save, and spend. The child distributes a portion of his income into each box. Thus a simple budget is established using visual control. When the box is empty, there is no money to spend. Even a six-year-old can understand this method.

Don't bail him out! His mistakes will be the best teacher.

By the time a child is 12, he is old enough to be exposed to the family's budget. He will understand that he is growing up because he can now share in making plans for spending the family income. He will realize that each member has a responsibility for wise spending, regardless of who provides the income. As the child matures, he should participate in every aspect of the family budget. It will help him to realize the extent and limitations of the family income as well as how to make the money stretch to meet the family's needs.

At first the child may think that the family has so much money that it is impossible to spend it all. To help him visualize the budget, have the family income converted to a sack of dollars. Place these on a table and divide the "income" pile into the various "expense" piles representing the categories of spending. It is often difficult for children to grasp numbers because they are abstract. The dollars will provide a tangible way for a child to understand the family budget.

The habit of saving should be established as soon as the child receives an income.

During the budget training, teach your child to become a wise consumer. Teach shopping skills, the ability to distinguish needs from wants and the fine art of waiting on the Lord to provide. Warn the child about the powerful influence of advertising and the danger of impulse spending.

When the child becomes a teenager, discontinue the allowance unless he presents a budget that accounts for how the last week's allowance was spent.

3. Giving

The best time to establish the personal habit of giving is when you are young. It is helpful for children to give a portion of their gifts to a tangible need they can visualize. For example, a child can understand the impact of his gift when his contribution is helping to construct the new church building, or when it is buying food for a needy family he knows.

Dr. Richard Halverson, former chaplain of the U.S. Senate, gave his son Chris this rich heritage as a child. Through a ministry that serves poor children, Chris and his brother gave money to support a Korean orphan named Kim who had lost his sight and an arm during the Korean War. Chris was taught to feel that Kim was his adopted brother. One Christmas, Chris bought Kim a harmonica. It was Kim's first personal possession. He cherished this gift from Chris and learned to play it well.

Today Kim is an evangelist, and in his presentation of the gospel he includes playing the harmonica. By being trained to give as a youth, Chris experienced firsthand the value of meeting people's needs and seeing God change lives as a result of faithful giving.

The best way for a child to become faithful in work is to establish the habit of daily household chores.

When your child is a teenager, a family or church mission trip to a Third World country can be a powerful experience. Direct exposure to abject poverty can initiate a lifetime of giving to the poor.

I also recommend a family time each week for dedicating that week's gifts to the Lord. It is important for the children to participate in this time of dedication and worship. The more involved children are with their parents in the proper handling of money, the better habits they will have as adults.

4. Saving and Investing

The habit of saving should be established as soon as the child receives an income. It is helpful to open a savings account for your child at this time. As the child matures, you also should expose him or her to various types of investments—stocks, bonds, real estate, etc.

Teach your children the benefits of compounding interest. If they grasp this concept and become faithful savers, they will enjoy financial stability as adults. Parents should demonstrate saving by doing so for something that will directly affect and benefit the children. A good example is a family vacation. Use a graph the children can fill in so they can chart the progress of the family's saving.

Children should have both short-term and long-term saving programs. The younger the child, the more important are short-term achievable goals. To a four-year-old, a week seems like a lifetime to save for a small purchase. He or she will not understand about saving for future education or retirement, but will get excited about saving for a small toy. Long-term saving for education, the first car, etc., should be a requirement. Some parents find it motivating to their child if they match their child's contribution to their long-term savings.

5. Debt

It is also important to teach the cost of money and how difficult it is to get out of debt. Dick Getty loaned his son and daughter the money to buy bicycles. Dick drew up a credit agreement with a schedule for repayment of the loan. He included the interest charged.

Strategy for independence

1- Verbally communicate biblical principles for handling money to your children.
2- Become models of financial faithfulness, allowing your children to observe closely how you apply these principles.
3- Create practical opportunities for children to experience God's financial principles.

After they successfully went through the long, difficult, process of paying off the loan, the family celebrated with a mortgage burning ceremony. Dick said that his children have appreciated those bikes more than any of their other possessions, and they have vowed to avoid debt in the future.

Learning experiences in money making

A father's advice:

Always do your best for your boss and he'll always have you back.

Because work is an essential element in becoming a faithful steward, parents have the responsibility to train each child in the value of work and proper work habits. If a child responds and learns how to work with a proper attitude, then he or she will not only have taken a giant step to becoming content, but he or she will become a valuable commodity in the job market. Good employees are difficult to find. Clearly, children need to learn the dignity and habit of work. There are four areas to consider in this training:

Training #1—Establish routine responsibilities

The best way for a child to become faithful in work is to establish the habit of daily household chores. For example, my daughter carries out the garbage and washed the dishes, and my son cleans the floors.

Training #2—Expose your children to your work

Not too many years ago most children were active participants in earning the family's money. They readily learned responsibility and the value of money. However, that is seldom the case today. Many children do not know how their father or mother earns the family income.

During a class several years ago, a participant said that he had asked his father what he did at work. "I make money," the father responded.

"For a long time," the participant said, "I thought my dad actually made dollar bills. My mother would ask Dad, 'How much did you draw this week?' I thought he was a great artist to be able to do all that detailed lettering and artwork."

An important way to teach the value of work is to expose the child to the parents' means of earning a living. If your children cannot visit you at work, at least take the time to explain your job to them. For those parents who manage their own businesses, children should be encouraged to actively participate.

One word of advice, because most children no longer are with their parents at work, the parents' work attitudes and habits around the home will be a major modeling influence. If a parent works hard at the office but complains about washing the dishes at home, what's being communicated to the children about work? Examine your work attitudes and activities at home to ensure that you are properly influencing your children to be godly workers.

> *"I have yet to meet an adult whose parents lived these biblical financial principles and also taught them systematically to their children."*
>
> *—Howard Dayton*

Training #3—Earn extra money at home

You should encourage your child to do extra work to earn money. A good rule of thumb is to pay the child a fair wage for the work you would have to hire someone else to do. For example, if your car needs washing and your daughter needs extra money and wants to wash it, let her. Be happy to pay her rather than the person at the car wash.

Training #4—Encourage your children to work for others

A paper route, baby-sitting, janitorial work, or waiting tables will serve as an education. A job gives children an opportunity to enter into an employee-employer relationship and to earn extra money.

As your child enters high school, it is a good idea to discontinue allowances during summer vacation. This will motivate him or her to earn their own money by holding a summer job. Moreover, some students can handle part-time work during the school year.

The objective of training your children in the value of work is to build and discipline their character. A working child with the proper attitude will be a more satisfied individual. He or she will grow up with more respect for the value of money and what is required to earn it.

(Howard Dayton, a graduate of Cornell University, is the founder and president of Crown Ministries. A former commercial real estate developer, he serves the ministry full-time at no salary. He is the author of Your Money Counts, Your Money, Frustration or Freedom?, and Getting out of Debt. He and his wife, Bev, live in Longwood, Florida, with their two children.)

Excerpted with permission from *Your Money Counts*, by Howard Dayton, published by Crown Ministries, Inc., 1996.

12

People Say They Want Riches

What they need is fulfillment of a purpose.

by John Mason

The world makes room for a man of purpose. His words and actions demonstrate that he knows where he is going.

You are built to conquer circumstances, solve problems and attain goals. You'll find no real satisfaction or happiness in life without obstacles to conquer, goals to achieve, and a purpose to accomplish. People say they want riches; what they need is fulfillment of a purpose. Happiness comes when we squander ourselves for a purpose.

If you aim for the top, you had better be prepared to land there.

In your heart there is a sleeping lion. Be on a mission. Have a definite sense of direction and purpose for your life. Successful lives are motivated by dynamic purpose. God can only bless your plan and direct you in accomplishing it if you have one. Strong convictions precede great actions.

Resigning yourself to fate

As soon as you resign yourself to fate, your resignation is promptly accepted. You don't have a fate; you have a purpose. When you look into the future, you'll see it's so bright it will make you squint. I'm encouraged by George Elliott, who said, "It's never too late to be what you might have been."

Laziness keeps on and on, but soon enough it arrives at poverty. We are weakest when we try to get something for nothing.

"More men fail through lack of purpose than lack of talent" (Billy Sunday). If your method is hit or miss, you'll usually miss.

"If you're not sure where you are going, you'll probably end up someplace else" (Robert F. Mager). Too many people don't know where they're going, but they're on their way. Growth for the sake of growth is the ideology of the cancer cell. Go forward with purpose.

Lord Chesterfield wrote: "Firmness of purpose is one of the most necessary sinews of character and one of the best instruments of success. Without it, genius wastes its efforts in a maze of inconsistencies."

Momentum doesn't just happen.

"The common conception is that motivation leads to action, but the reverse is true—action precedes motivation" (Robert McKain). "Don't wait to be motivated. Take the bull by the horns until you have him screaming for mercy." (Michael Cadena)

You are sure to find another cross if you flee the one you are to carry. The man who has no direction is slave of his circumstances. The poorest man is not he who is without a cent, but he who is without purpose. "The only thing some people do is grow older" (Ed Howe).

"If you don't have a vision for your life, then you probably haven't focused in on anything" (Dr. David Burns). In the absence of vision there can be no clear and constant focus.

Once your purpose is clear, decisions will jump at you. "When you discover your mission, you will feel its demand. It will fill you with enthusiasm and a burning desire to get to work on it" (W. Clement Stone).

Along the road towards your destiny, remember: nothing great is created suddenly.

A man of words and not of deeds is like a flower bed full of weeds. Don't let weeds grow around your dreams.

Little is Big

One of the most common prayers I pray for others (and myself) is this: "Lord, please send small opportunities across their paths to do what you've called them to do." When we're faithful in those small opportunities, God says to us, "You have been faithful in handling this small amount ... so now I will give you many more responsibilities. Begin the joyous tasks I have assigned to you" (Matt. 25:21, TLB).

People who think they are too big to do little things are perhaps too little to be asked to do big things. Small opportunities are often the beginning of great enterprises.

Nothing great is created suddenly. Nothing can be done except little by little. Within that little thing lies a big opportunity. Small things make a big difference; therefore, do all that it takes to be successful in little things.

You will never do great things if you can't do small things in a great way. All difficult things have their beginning in that which is easy, and great things in that which is small. One of the major differences between people who have momentum and those who don't, is that those who do, pay attention to their small ideas and opportunities.

"You can't build a reputation on what you're going to do."

—Henry Ford

Courage to begin

The courage to begin is the same courage it takes to succeed. That courage separates dreamers from achievers. The beginning is the most important part of any endeavor. Worse than a quitter is the person who is afraid to begin. Ninety percent of success is showing up and starting. You may be disappointed if you fail, but you are doomed if you don't try.

Don't be deceived: knowledge of a path can never be a substitute for putting one foot in front of the other. Discover step by step excitement. Robert Schuller sums it up: "Winning starts with beginning."

The first step is the hardest. "That's why many fail—they don't get started—they don't go. They don't overcome inertia. They don't begin" (W. Clement Stone).

Dare to begin. No endeavor is worse than that which is not attempted. You don't know what you can do until you have tried. People, like trees, must grow or wither. There's no standing still. Do what you can. "It is always your next move" (N. Hill).

(John Mason, founder and president of Insight International, is an author and popular speaker at numerous churches and conferences throughout the Unites States and abroad. His best-selling books include An Enemy Called Average, You're Born An Original—Don't Die A Copy!, Know

Your Limits, Then Ignore Them, and several others. His most recent book is Why Ask Why: If You Know the Right Questions, You Can Find the Right Answers, published by Bridge-Logos Publishers.)

Excerpted with permission from *Let Go of Whatever Makes You Stop*, by John L. Mason, published by Insight International, 1994.

IV

Saving With A
Purpose

13

Three Steps Closer to a Financial Plan

Three steps forward in planning your financial future may not seem like much, but the average person hasn't moved yet.

by Scott Kays, CFP

All of us have an unlimited number of alternatives to which we can allocate our finances. We have things we would like to do, ministries to which we would like to give, and items we would like to buy, all of which cost money. When helping clients formulate financial goals, one of the first questions I normally ask is "When would you like to retire?" The typical response is "Yesterday."

Typical question: "When would you like to retire?"

Typical answer: "Yesterday."

The problem that the vast majority of us share is that we have a limited amount of financial resources to meet our financial desires. This creates the necessity of using our limited resources as efficiently as possible. To do so, we must determine the goals that are most important to us. If I cannot do everything I would like to do, I should at least strive to accomplish the objectives that are most important to me.

Three general steps in the planning process

Step #1. Set goals

The first step in developing any plan is to set goals. Determine what it is that you want to accomplish. This defines the reason for the very existence of the plan itself. Financial goals should be reasonable, and, very important, they should be measurable. If goals are not stated in measurable terms, then they are vague, and it will be difficult to know when they have been accomplished. Vague goals will not provide the proper motivation for their achievement.

Years ago I heard of a study that had been conducted to determine what it is that makes financially successful people successful. The researcher interviewed hundreds of people from various walks of life and socio-economic backgrounds. After conducting extensive research, he stratified people into three categories. He classified approximately 58 percent of the subjects as having achieved average levels of financial success. Next, he delineated an upper 13 percent of participants, who he classified as having attained above average levels of financial success. Of that top 13 percent, he deemed the top 3 percent to be extremely successful.

Three general steps in the planning process

1. *Set goals*
2. *Determine your current position*
3. *Develop a step-by-step written plan*

His first task was to determine the most prevalent characteristics of the top 13 percent of subjects. He discovered that one of the most common qualities of that group was they were goal-setters. They knew what they wanted to accomplish in life. They were

The secret of the top 3% —they wrote down their goals!

living life with a purpose, instead of just existing from day to day. As a result, they expended their efforts in directions that led to the achievement of their goals.

He determined that the second most prevalent characteristic of the upper 13 percent was that they were planners. They not only had concrete goals defining what they wanted to accomplish, but they took the time to plan how they would achieve those goals. Each morning when they woke up, they had a reason for living that day; they had specific tasks they needed to carry out.

The researcher's next duty was to determine, out of the 13 percent above average group, what characteristics separated the top 3 percent (extremely successful people) from the remaining 10 percent. What was it that allowed them to go beyond their colleagues and achieve levels of success about which most people only dream? *The primary characteristic he discovered these people shared was that they wrote their goals down!*

The power of goal setting is awesome! When we take the extra time to write our goals down and let these written goals serve as a constant visual reminder of where our efforts need to be focused, the power of goal setting becomes even greater.

Step #2. Determine Your Current Position

Determining where you want to go and setting specific goals are critical to the development of a plan, but equally important is determining your starting point. This step answers the question, "What do you have to work with that is going to help you achieve your objectives?"

For most people, the two primary resources available to them are their current income and their current assets. Their discretionary income should be directed into those areas that will help them attain their goals most efficiently. Discretionary income, by the way, is one's income after all his or her obligatory payments are made, such as taxes, mortgage payments, and other debt payments.

The same is true for one's assets. All too often I meet people in my office who state that their primary desire is to grow their assets for retirement purposes, and, yet, when I examine their current assets, most of their investments are designed to generate income, not growth. When your assets are not lined up with your goals, this results in inefficient money—money that does not work hard for you; its potential is not being fully utilized.

Successfully achieving financial independence requires the elimination of insufficient money. We must get all of our current assets to work their hardest for us, as well as direct a portion of our income stream into investments that will help us achieve our goals most efficiently.

Step #3. Develop a Step-by-Step Written Plan

Once you know where you are and where you want to go, the next phase is to develop a step-by-step written plan to get you from point A to point B. This written plan should outline the action steps necessary to achieve the desired goal, as well as specify a time frame within which each step should be taken. Milestones should be built into the plan so that your progress can be measured on a regular, periodic basis.

These are the same three steps that you would follow in planning a two-week vacation. You would take out a map, circle your destination, circle your starting point, and then map out the shortest route from the starting point to the destination. The sad truth is that most people will take more

Most people will take more time to plan a two-week vacation than they will to plan their entire life's financial affairs.

time to plan a two-week vacation than they will to plan their entire life's financial affairs.

The first financial planning case I ever worked on was for a group of doctors preparing for retirement, all of whom had been making six-digit incomes for many years. I would have expected that they could have retired anytime they wanted to. The results of their financial analyses were so startling to me that the need for planning was indelibly etched into my consciousness.

One doctor, who was in his early sixties and desirous of retiring immediately, was told that he would have to continue practicing medicine a few more years in order to enjoy the retirement lifestyle he desired. Another was forced to sell his home and move to a smaller residence in order to reduce his living expenses to a level that would allow him to quit working. Why would doctors who had maintained such a high level of income for so many years be subject to such disappointing news regarding their goals for retirement? Because, in spite of their substantial incomes, they had never taken the time to ensure they were setting aside enough assets to support them in their retirement years.

Without a financial plan, a six-figure income will not be adequate preparation for retirement.

How to pay off your mortgage early

Let's say that you have made the decision to pay off your mortgage early. How do you accomplish this? Generally, advisers recommend that you dispose of your mortgage early by making an additional principal payment each month along with your regular house payment. Another frequently suggested method is to pay half your mortgage payment every two weeks, resulting in an extra house payment each year. I do not recommend either method.

Assume that you make an extra principal payment each month on your mortgage. Eventually, you reduce the loan balance by $30,000 more than you would have by making normal monthly payments. Then, unexpectedly, your company downsizes. You lose your job, and you find yourself unable to make your mortgage payment for a few months. No problem, you think, since you have paid an extra $30,000 on your mortgage balance. The mortgage company will be understanding and allow you to skip a few payments. Right?

Unfortunately, that is not the way it works. Paying extra on your mortgage does not buy you the right to skip any payments during financially difficult times. The lender expects each payment to be made in a timely fashion. If you begin skipping payments, the lender has the right to foreclose on your home and sell it at whatever price it can procure in order to recover its money. Your extra mortgage payments have only afforded your lender the luxury of selling your house for a cheaper price to get all its money back. The lender appreciates that you were kind enough to build up the extra equity in your home.

> There is nothing wrong with paying your mortgage off early. Just do it in such a way that increases your security, not the lender's security.

A better solution

Let me offer a better solution. If you decide to pay your house off early, make an extra principal payment each month, but make these payments to a liquid investment account, such as a mutual fund, not to the mortgage company. Continue making these additional payments to your investment account until the balance in this account equals the balance of your mortgage. Then pay off the mortgage in its entirety.

By abolishing your home loan in this manner, you will have liquid funds with which to make house payments for an extended period of time before the loan is fully paid, if that becomes necessary. If you instead pay the mortgage down gradually, the extra money will be illiquid and unavailable for making monthly payments during an emergency. In the above example, had you kept $30,000 liquid, you would not have lost your home during your period of unemployment.

Another advantage to this technique is that it allows you to earn stock market returns on your money instead of merely saving mortgage interest expenses. Assuming that the stock market continues earning historical rates of return, which are substantially higher than mortgage rates, this would allow you to liquidate your mortgage even faster. The obvious assumption behind the successful use of this technique, of course, is that you do not dip into your accumulated funds for anything other than an emergency.

There is nothing wrong with paying your mortgage off early. Just do it in such a way that increases *your* security, not the *lender's* security.

Imagine paying off your mortgage in one lump payment!

(Scott Kays is a respected expert in the field of financial planning. He is President and Founder of Kays Financial Advisory Corporation, an Atlanta based management firm. He frequently holds investment seminars, and is author of Achieving Your Financial Potential, Doubleday, 1999. He lives in Atlanta with his wife and four children.)

Excerpted with permission from *Achieving Your Financial Potential* by Scott Kays, CFP, published by Doubleday, 1999.

14

Wealth Secrets of Wise Millionaires

How to master financial success without becoming a slave to money.

by Peter Lowe

Many people think that becoming rich is an impossible dream. When they picture millionaires, they think of big spenders living lavish, glamorous, lifestyles. The average millionaire is a very different sort of person.

According to financial consultant, Tod Barnhart, the average self-made millionaire is a "middle-aged (or older) person who drives a moderately-priced car... has been married twenty years or more to the same person, goes to church, owns or runs a business, has kids or grandkids, works ten hours a day and loves it." In other words, the typical American millionaire is an ordinary person who has achieved wealth and success over time, by working, planning and saving for it. You can do the same.

> *The typical millionaire is an ordinary person who has achieved wealth and success over time, by working, planning and saving for it.*

Our free enterprise system creates opportunities, and gives us the freedom to take advantage of them. No matter what your background, you can become a millionaire. These six secrets have brought extraordinary success to seemingly ordinary people. They can do the same for you.

1. Treat money as a servant, not a master

A misplaced focus on money can actually thwart financial success. As playwright Henrik Ibsen concluded, "Money brings you food but not appetite, medicine but not health, acquaintance but not friends, servants but not loyalty, days of joy, but not peace or happiness."

Three best habits to increase Wealth

1- Spend less than you earn
2- Form a savings plan
3- Invest your savings

Financial consultant Robert Ringer cautions in his book, *Million Dollar Habits*, "Instead of possessing money, what happens when an individual's goal is money is that he becomes possessed by money. Instead of keeping money in perspective, it becomes an obsession."

Far too many people have sacrificed their health to gain wealth, only to spend their wealth trying to regain their health. A proper outlook on money is needed to become— and remain—healthy, wealthy and wise.

2. Form wealthy habits

Have you ever wondered how some people become wealthy so easily? No matter what they do, money seems to gravitate to them. They have learned the millionaires' secret of making a habit of making money. Tod Barnhart wrote in his book, *The Five Rituals of Wealth*, "I've found one thing to be absolutely true of those who control vast resources: they don't just do wealthy things once in awhile when they feel like it. They habitually live in a state of wealth. They save, dream, plan, invest, and give in a never-ending cycle."

> "Most people don't have a plan--they operate day to day and paycheck to paycheck."
> —*Joseph Plumeri, Primerica Chairman*

What are the habits of wealth? Here are the three most important habits you can adopt to build a foundation of wealth and financial security.

A. Spend less than you earn

The first habit of wealth is to make the best use of the financial resources you already have. No matter what your salary, you should make it a habit to spend less than you earn.

Six secrets to
develop wealth

1. Treat money as a servant, not a master
2. Form wealthy habits
   A. Spend less than you earn
   B. Form a savings plan
   C. Invest your savings
3. Find work you love
4. Set goals for your desired outcomes
5. Shun shady schemes
6. Increase your knowledge

Everyone can reduce their expenditures without making a significant dent in their lifestyles. I challenge you to account for every dollar you spent last month. How much of it was necessary? How much was important? If you are like most people, doing a personal audit of your purchases for even one month will reveal that you wound up spending a lot of money on things you didn't need, didn't really want, and may not even like.

B. Form a savings plan

Once you get your spending under control, you can form a savings plan, and begin to track your growing wealth. Wealth is measured by how much you keep, not how much you make. Every time you receive a paycheck, set aside a portion of it to keep—preferably, ten percent or more.

C. Invest your savings

Hoarding money will make you a miser, not a millionaire. The essence of investment is to generate wealth—creating opportunities for others and to share in the wealth created. The more, and more wisely, you invest, the more wealth you create for yourself and others.

3. Find work you love

I am convinced that the surest—and most fun—way to succeed financially is to love your work. Most of America's millionaires made their fortune not by running after profit, but by throwing themselves into work they adored. They viewed their work as a mission, and riches became a by-product.

4. Set goals for your desired outcomes

The famous, multi-millionaire Napoleon Hill, who wrote down Andrew

Develop values early

J.C. Penny, department store executive raised on a Missouri farm, heard his father say, "Love your neighbor as yourself, and never forsake the Golden Rule." Jim Moran, the automobile giant raised in Chicago, said his mother taught him her values: "Be on time, keep your word, don't take what doesn't belong to you, and if you do anything, do it right."

(Excerpted from True Wealth ... By the Book, John Beehner, published by The Book Publishing, 1999)

116

Carnegie's secrets to wealth in his best-seller, *Think and Grow Rich*, put it this way: "There is one quality which one must possess to win, and that is definiteness of purpose, the knowledge of what one wants, and a burning desire to possess it."

5. Shun shady schemes

The quickest way to destroy your fortune and reputation is to engage in unwise or unethical deals and practices. No matter how wealthy you are, your wealth is never secure unless it has been built on a foundation of integrity. Many of the richest men in America—Ivan Boesky and Michael Milkin, for example— have seen their financial empires disintegrate overnight because of unethical practices.

No matter how wealthy you are, your wealth is never secure unless it has been built on a foundation of integrity.

6. Increase your knowledge

Knowledge not only brings high yields, it is invulnerable to inflation, impervious to recession, and totally unaffected by stock market crashes. Material possessions, stocks and bonds, and liquid assets can be stolen, lost or destroyed; but the sum of your wisdom, expertise and abilities are yours to keep forever. As the great entrepreneur Henry Ford stated, "If money is your hope for independence, you will never have it. The only real security that a man can have is a reserve of knowledge, experience, and ability."

"There is no excuse why everyone, if he acquires the knowledge early enough, should not retire a millionaire."
—*Dave Ramsey*

No matter what your current financial situation, you can put the wealth secrets of millionaires to work for you. The knowledge, habits and practices that have helped them amass a fortune can also make your money multiply—and even make you a millionaire!

(Peter Lowe, raised in Pakistan and India as a missionary kid, is one of the most notable success and motivational speakers ever. His Peter Lowe International success seminars draw more than 300,000 in attendance each year. He resides in Tampa with his wife and partner, Tamara, and their two sons.)

15

Saving for Wealth

Why compound interest can be your best friend.

by Dave Ramsey

Money is active. Most consumers do not understand how quickly time, interest rates, and payments work for them or against them. At work on your money is a mathematical monster called compound interest. Compound interest can either be your best friend financially, if you make it work for you, or your worst possible enemy, if it works against you. If you are saving at good interest rates, every month, and for many years, compound interest is your best friend, however, if you have borrowed over long periods of time at high interest rates, you see it as your worst enemy.

Compound interest can either be your best friend or your worst possible enemy.

Mathematically speaking, compound interest works exponentially or in a geometric progression. In English, this simply means that your money is affected by mathematical multiplied explosion, not by simple addition, such as 1+1=2.

If you will look at the payment schedule on your house or your car, you will see how the first bunch of payments are almost all interest and how you have paid back almost no debt. That is compound interest working against you. But it can also work just as strongly for you.

119

Watch closely now

If you start to save at age twenty-five with the idea that you will withdraw your money at age sixty-five, you will save for forty years. Let's say that you put $1,000 in a savings account one time at age twenty-five, and you never deposit or withdraw anything from that account (you just let the interest compound or grow) until age sixty-five.

The real numbers

At 6 percent per year you would have just over $10,000 at age sixty-five, so if we double the interest rate to 12 percent you should have around $16,000, right? *Wrong!* You will have just over $93,000 at 12 percent at age sixty-five.

That is compound interest working for you—it's a multiplication effect rather than an addition effect that most may have thought. Now let's raise the rate of interest again—to 18 percent—and what will we have? $750,378!

Here's the comparison:

· $1,000 one-time investment

· No withdrawal

· Age 25 to age 65 (40 years)

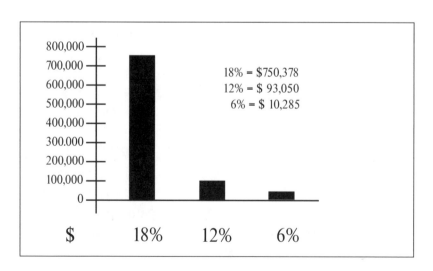

18% = $750,378
12% = $ 93,050
6% = $ 10,285

Can you see that the rate and term at which you save or borrow is very important? Now let see how banks make a profit.

Do you have a bank credit card? Do you also have a savings account with that bank? Many people loan the bank their money in a savings account at 6 percent or less and then borrow their own money back by having a credit card balance and paying 18 percent.

If you left $1,000 in a savings account like this and kept a $1,000 balance on your credit card, the bank will have made the spread at virtually no risk and with no investment for a $740,093 profit for every time this happens in our forty-year example. If you multiply this scenario times thousands of customers, it is enough to make you understand how the banks own most of the tall buildings in every major city.

Now you understand how the banks own most of the tall buildings in every major city.

A little bit goes a long way

To further show you how important the understanding of compound interest is and its power in your finances, let's look at retirement. Suppose you started at age twenty and saved for forty-five years until age sixty-five, saving only $65 per month at 12 percent average annual return (which a long-term growth mutual fund could easily do). In forty years you would accumulate $1,394,555 for retirement.

You must, however, save it every month. Saving is like planting an oak tree. You cannot keep pulling it by the roots to check its progress. There is no excuse why everyone, if they acquire the knowledge early enough, should not retire a millionaire. Compound interest is powerful, and remember, it works for or against you, with equal power.

Wow, what a car!

Joe and Sue bought a $16,000 car for $300 per month. If they had waited and bought a $5,400 car for $100 per month and saved $200 per month at 10 percent for seven years, they would have $24,190 at the end. As long as they stay on their plan, they will have car payments for the rest of their lives, with compound interest working against them.

Using my second plan, however, we can imagine the scenario years into the future. By year seven the car is junk, in either plan, but suppose they saved that $24,190. Then they bought a $16,000 car for cash from that savings, leaving them $8,190.

Again, the best way to get rich quick is not to get rich quick, but to watch your decisions and let time make you wealthy.

The new car

Joe and Sue now have a new car with no car payment and $8,190 in the bank, but let's go yet another seven years. They have no car payment, so instead of the $100 payment and the $200 per month they were doing each month, now they decide just to save $100 per month, freeing up $200 per month.

At the end of seven more years, that $8,190 left over plus $100 per month plus 10 percent interest will now grow to $28,539. Now they again have a seven-year-old car that is worthless, so they buy yet another $16,000 car for cash, leaving $12,539 in savings. For another seven years they have no car payment and, though they do no additional saving, the $12,539 at 10 percent will grow to $24,436!

Pay me now or pay me big later

That is a hard chain of events to follow. The bottom line is that if Joe and Sue would sacrifice with a lesser purchase up-front and save the difference, and then continue the process, they will be driving *paid-for* cars and have savings the rest of their lives.

> *Saving is like planting an oak tree. You cannot keep pulling it by the roots to check its progress.*

That is compound interest working for you. Again, the best way to get rich quick is *not* to get rich quick, but to watch your decisions and let time make you wealthy.

This idea—saving a certain monthly amount with interest in order to have the amount needed to make your purchases—is called "a sinking fund." The concept of a sinking fund is simple. It is making payments in reverse.

If you want $4,000 for a dining room suite, why don't you use a sinking fund savings program instead of borrowing it at 24 percent? You can save $151 per month for 24 months at 10 percent—and then pay cash. (Note: $151 times 24 is only $3,624. The rest is interest in your favor.)

But if you financed the dining room suite at 24 percent at the furniture store, you would have paid $151 for 31 months, for a total of $4,681 for the same suite, not to mention the discount you should get for flashing cash.

All you need to design a sinking fund for any purchase is a simple financial calculator, or your banker can probably help you figure out your program, especially if you are saving in his bank. You need to always remember to make the power of compound interest work for you.

Who is the smarter—*Ben* or *Arthur?*

Bernard Zick, who has a master's degree in business administration (MBA) and is an expert in the time value of money, gave this consumer quiz in his monthly newsletter:

Once you have your emergency fund of three to six months' expenses in place, you should begin to look at diversifying.

Ben, age twenty-two, invests $1,000 per year compounded annually at 10 percent for eight years until he is thirty years old. For the next thirty-five years, until he is sixty-five, Ben invests not one penny more.

Arthur, age thirty, invests $1,000 per year for thirty-five years until he is sixty-five years old. His investment also earns 10 percent compound interest per year. At age sixty-five, will Arthur or Ben have the most money?

The answer in the chart below is yet another example that strongly shows the power of compound interest and the importance of getting started *now*.

AGE	BEN INVESTS		ARTHUR INVESTS	
22	1,000	1,100	0	0
23	1.000	2,310	0	0
24	1,000	3,641	0	0
25	1,000	5,105	0	0
26	1,000	6,716	0	0
27	1,000	8,487	0	0
28	1,000	10,436	0	0
29	1,000	12,579	0	0
30	0	13,837	1,000	1,100
31	0	15,221	1,000	2,310
32	0	16,743	1,000	3,641

33	0	18,418	1,000	5,105
34	0	20,259	1,000	6,716
35	0	22,285	1,000	8,487
36	0	24,514	1,000	10,436
37	0	26,965	1,000	12,579
38	0	29,662	1,000	14,937
39	0	32,628	1,000	17,531
40	0	35,891	1,000	20,384
41	0	39,480	1,000	23,523
42	0	43,428	1,000	26,975
43	0	47,771	1,000	30,772
44	0	52,548	1,000	34,950
45	0	57,802	1,000	39,545
46	0	63,583	1,000	44,599
47	0	69,941	1,000	50,159
48	0	76,935	1,000	56,275
49	0	84,628	1,000	63,002
50	0	93,091	1,000	70,403
51	0	102,400	1,000	78,543
52	0	112,640	1,000	87,497
53	0	123,904	1,000	97,347
54	0	136,295	1,000	108,182
55	0	149,924	1,000	120,100
56	0	164,917	1,000	133,210
57	0	181,409	1,000	147,631
58	0	199,549	1,000	163,494
59	0	219,504	1,000	180,943
60	0	241,455	1,000	200,138
61	0	265,600	1,000	221,252
62	0	292,160	1,000	244,477
63	0	321,376	1,000	270,024
64	0	353,514	1,000	298,127
65	0	**388,865**	1,000	**329,039**

Eggs in a basket

Once you have your emergency fund of three to six months' expenses in place, you should begin to look at diversifying. The financial community calls this not putting all your eggs in one basket (probably because sometimes the financial community drops the basket). The concept of spreading your investments to avoid risk is very good.

After you have your foundation laid, you should be careful not to leave all or the majority of your wealth in one institution or even in one type of investment. You should be careful not to attempt to get too fancy too soon. Unless you have at least $15,000, you can just keep it in your local bank or money market and be boring. But if you are saving actively and applying some of these principles, you very quickly will have more than that to watch over.

As of this writing, you are insured in FDIC banks up to $100,000 per individual, but you should not have all of your funds in one institution. If your FDIC bank fails—and many of them have—you will get your money. The problem is that it may be months or even years before the FDIC pays on the bank's insurance. So you should never bank in only one place. (Your banker will not like that advice!)

You should also never have all your money in real estate or the stock market or money markets or in any one place. As your cash stash increases, you can get very sophisticated in your approach, but always remember that simplicity will usually win out over even the most learned advice when it comes to personal money management.

(Dave Ramsey had accumulated over four million dollars in real estate by age 26, then lost it all. His financial life has since been rebuilt. He is founder of The Lampo Group, a counseling firm created to do bankruptcy avoidance counseling. He is a best-selling author, radio host, and speaker. He lives in Tennessee with his wife and three children.)

(Excerpted with permission from *Financial Peace*, by Dave Ramsey, Viking Penguin, 1997.)

16

Seven Secrets to Increasing Your Wealth

The greatest wealth secrets are not secrets, they are simply principles not followed.

by Darrin Smith

What you are about to read is known by approximately 1/10 of 1% of the entrepreneurs and professionals worldwide. The individuals who embrace these principles often generate enormous wealth for themselves and the people they love most. The secret is not in the *Take advantage of every opportunity, and do not procrastinate.* secret itself, but rather in the implementing of the principle. After all, as they say, "Easier said than done."

1. Work hard

The man who will not work, should not eat. A good work ethic is paramount to achieving any type of success in life. Implicit in a good work ethic is hard work.

First, set strong and definite goals to work towards. And, for each goal you set for yourself, break them down into smaller tasks. Be mindful to complete each task that you set for yourself. Become a person of action and seize each moment. Take advantage of every opportunity, and do not procrastinate.

Second, you must desire to succeed because desire precedes all accomplishments. The hungrier you are for success, the clearer your mind will work, and you will become more sensitive to each opportunity that presents itself. With each desire to accomplish, determination will serve as your impetus. Determination will pave the way to success.

Third, dispel the myth that only those who are lucky succeed. You don't have to be lucky to succeed, for luck is nothing more than hard work.

Fourth, disregard the adage that work is a curse. Work is for you to enjoy. If you work diligently and wisely, and invest your earnings, you will succeed. Even a woodpecker owes his success to the fact that he uses his head and keeps pecking away until he finishes the job he started.

Fifth, you possess all that is required to obtain all that you desire. Therefore, when you bargain with life, do not sell yourself short.

My Wage

I bargained with Life for a penny,
and Life would pay no more,
however I begged at evening
when I counted my scanty score.

For Life is a just employer,
He gives you what you ask,
but once you have set the wages,
why, you must bear the task.
I worked for a menial's hire,

only to learn, dismayed,

that any wage I had asked of Life,

Life would have paid.

(Jessie B. Rittenhouse)

2. Manage your wealth

Wealth grows for the one who learns not to spend wantonly what he has earned. With your wealth, give 1/10th of it to God. This is not a one-time act, continue it as long as you continue to make money. You ask, what is the wisdom in giving? Not only does the Bible command it, but consider the palm of a hand that is full of sand. The tighter you hold the sand, the more it seeps out, and nothing replaces it. However, if you slowly open your palm, some sand may blow away, but most will remain. Moreover, the palm is open to receive more. Your giving of your ten percent resembles more of an investment that opens your palm for many returns.

Next, you must save and invest at least 1/10 of the wealth that you acquire. The remaining 8/10 is available for your use. Nevertheless, spend wisely. Control your expenditures; differentiate between needs and wants. Your appetite often surpasses your earning capacity. What you regard as necessary expenses will always surpass your earnings. Therefore, discipline yourself to satisfy only the bare necessities of life and some of your wants, but never expending more than eighty percent of your earnings.

What you regard as necessary expenses will always surpass your earnings.

The more wealth that you accumulate, the more readily it comes and increases in quantity. The wealth that you accumulate earns more, its earnings earn more, and the growth continues.

Remember, a percentage of your earning is yours to keep. A minimum of one-tenth is recommended. A penny

129

saved is a penny earned, and each penny saved is a vehicle to work for you. Each additional penny it earns also becomes your vehicle to increase your earnings. If you want to become wealthy, then what you save must reap dividends, and its earnings must also earn. Eventually, it will bring you the prosperity that you seek.

3. Invest wisely

Invest soundly, since wealth labors diligently and contentedly for the one who finds for it profitable employment. The reward is abundant multiplication.

When you start to accumulate wealth, your opportunity to increase profitability is sure to come. And, as the years pass, this wealth will increase in surprising fashion. Be wise and delay in your expectation of an instant return. A small and safe return is more desirable than risk. Promises of large rates of return are deceitful sirens that ring-out and lure the unwise into the pasture of loss and remorse.

Counsel with the wise. Seek the advice of those who are shrewd in handling wealth. Don't jeopardize your treasure, but preserve it by being content with consistent increase. Your wealth is not measured in what you currently possess, but in the income that you build. Therefore, seek to build a stream of income that continues to flow whether you are at work or play. Wealth harbors within the bosom of the one who invests it under the advice of the wise. Seek the advice of these whose daily work is handling wealth.

4. Guard your wealth

Guard your treasure from loss. Wealth slips away from the one who invests it in a business or purpose that he is unfamiliar with, or in an investment that is not approved of by those who are skilled in sound investments.

If you have obtained wealth, but lack proper financial management, you will perceive any whim as an opportunity for sound investment. Seek the counsel of wise financial investors, who possess a proven track record, to analyze the potential profit margin of your investment. If you are unskilled in the area of financial investment, you should not trust your own judgment. Frequently your judgment is imperfect, and your inexperience may cost you your wealth.

Enticing propositions with promises of overnight success come to the wealthy. Therefore, seek the counsel of wise financial planners who will discover the risk factor that hide behind every plan that promises to make great wealth suddenly.

Guard your wealth from loss by investing only where your wealth is protected, and where it may be reclaimed when desired and still returns a profit. Secure the advice of those experienced in the area, and let their wisdom protect your treasure form unsafe investment.

Seven Secrets to increasing your wealth

1 Work hard
2 Manage your wealth
3 Invest wisely
4 Guard your wealth
5 Ownership is paramount
6 Lead wisely
7 Insure a future income

Wealth flees the one who:

· Forces it to impossible earnings,

· Follows the alluring advice of tricksters and schemers, and

· Trusts it to his or her own inexperience and romantic notions of investing.

5. Ownership is paramount

Now that you have acquired some wealth, paid your tithe, enjoyed some and invested the rest, it is time to own a piece of the pie. Start by making your house a profitable investment, and own your own home.

Next, pay your debt with all the promptness that is within your power. Plan a debt reducing strategy. Do not try to reduce all your debt at once. Pay in small consistent sums, showing partiality to none. Continue to pay your tithes, being also mindful to retain a portion for your enjoyment even as you strive to reduce your debt. And, continue to invest your wealth in such a manner that it earns you more.

There are two ways of being rich. The first is to have all you want, the second is to be satisfied with what you have.

Do not avoid your debts. It is easier to pay one's debts than to avoid them. A word to the wise: do not purchase things that you are unable to pay for at that moment.

6. Lend wisely

Do not risk undertaking a loan if you cannot guarantee payment. Just because your wealth will facilitate more opportunity to render aid to others, you must render help wisely. It is fine to assist those who are in trouble or to help those who have been overtaken by misfortune. It is also good to give people a start in life, that they may progress and become valuable citizens, but in your desire to help, employ wisdom. Do not take on the burden that belongs to others.

If you lend, lend in such a way that it may earn you more, and lend with caution in a variety of places. Furthermore, if you have attained wealth to the point that you can spare, then offer your wealth to the labor of others. But,

A Recipe for Success...
Bear in mind these
salient points:

• *First, what success means—the successful doing, the doing well of whatever you do in whatever position you're in.*
• *Second, the price of success—hard work, patience, and a few sacrifices.*
• *Third, in religious life—a firm unwavering belief in God and in prayer, and a life consistent with that belief for yourself and for others.*
• *Fourth, in social life—moderation.*
• *Fifth, in marriage—love.*
• *Sixth, in business—thoroughness; not thoroughness alone in large things or what is apparent to the eye, but thoroughness in all things, not slightly small things.*

(Paraphrased from Edward Bok)

do not risk losing the wealth for which you have labored and sacrificed in order to secure others. Do not lend if you are not confident that the loan is safe and that it will be repaid to you. Also, never lend wealth where you are not convinced that its commission will be promptly repaid to you.

Furthermore, avoid the fantastic plans of impractical people who think they see ways to invest your money to make unusually large earnings. These plans are the creations of dreamers who are unskilled in the safe and dependable laws of sound investment. Be conservative in what you expect to earn in order that you may keep and enjoy your wealth. To loan with a promise of extremely high returns is to invite loss.

Money is the merchandise of the lender. It is easy to lend. However, if it is not lent wisely, it is impossible to retrieve.

7. Insure a future income

One of the most important reasons for obtaining wealth is to make preparation for a suitable income in the future. Plan your investments that they may endure safely for years to come. And, invest in such a way that your investment will be available when the necessity or retirement arrives.

You cannot afford to delay in insuring future income for old age and the protection of your family, no matter how prosperous your investments and business may be today.

You cannot afford to delay in insuring future income for old age and the protection of your family, no matter how prosperous your investments and business may be today. Provide in advance for the needs of your golden years and the protection of your family. The person who acquires and keeps wealth is good to his family, while the person who fails to acquire wealth or loses wealth is disloyal to his or her family.

Make the necessary estate planning, via will or trust, to ensure smooth, proper, and honorable division of your wealth. Increase knowledge, cultivate your power to become wiser by studying, and acknowledge the areas of your ignorance, then seek wise counsel to help.

Finally, secure a variety of insurance policies such as life, health, mortgage, etc. This guards you against the unexpected tragedies of life. You cannot afford to be without adequate protection.

Two ways of being rich

There are two ways of being rich. The first is to have all you want, the second is to be satisfied with what you have.

In sum, learn to live upon less than you earn. Learn to seek the advice from those who have gained competence through their own experiences. Learn to let your wealth work for you. Enjoy life while you are here. Do not try to save too much. If one-tenth of your gross earnings is all you can comfortably save, then be content. Live within your means and don't become too miserly and afraid to spend. Life is to be enjoyed.

(Darrin Smith has been in pro football since 1993. He is founder and president of Millionaires United, which provides its members with the training, motivation, and networking necessary to be better business owners, investors, entrepreneurs, and more.)

V

Investing for the Future

17

Investment Tips for Beginners

Since there are no false starts in investing, whoever starts first usually wins in the end.

by R. Richard Everett

Investing for the first time can be scary, intimidating, and downright nerve-racking. No one wants to lose all their hard-earned money to a bad investment—and yet, novice or first-time investors have been known to do strange and foolish things. I have met people who have never invested before and suddenly they buy a start-up company because they heard a hot tip down at the barber shop, or they buy stock they know nothing or little about because Uncle Harry was talking about it at the latest social gathering.

It's amazing to see the kind of research that goes into purchasing a new television or refrigerator; yet, we blindly throw our money into a stock with little or no research. I have encountered several individuals who lend to or invest with a family member or close friend to open a new restaurant, retail store, or manufacturing

The "hot tip" at the barber shop has led to many foolish investments.

operation—with virtually no research. Granted, some of these opportunities occasionally work out, but most do not. Unfortunately, the first-time investor loses everything and never attempts to invest again—and that's too bad.

Investing, speculating, or gambling?

There is an immense difference between investing, speculating, and gambling. The scenarios previously mentioned are speculating and gambling, not investing. Investing can be both rewarding and exciting, if done properly. Think about this—the Dow Jones Industrial Average (DJIA), an index* to measure how well or poorly the stock market has done, was at 40 in 1929 (just after the stock market crash that lead into the Great Depression). In 1999, the DJIA peaked at 11,400. Doing some quick math, that's over a 17,000% increase! In conjunction with this, the average annual compounded rate of return for the Dow over the past 100 years is just shy of 12%—not bad! *(*It is not possible to invest directly in an index and past performance may not be indicative of future returns.)*

Having given you two astounding statistics, I ask the question—How could anyone have lost money in the stock market? Looking back to 1987 (the second stock market crash of this century), the Dow has more than quadrupled. That's correct—theoretically, you would have doubled your money twice in less than 15 years.

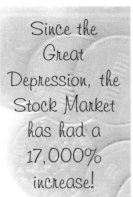

Since the Great Depression, the Stock Market has had a 17,000% increase!

In order to take advantage of the incredible growth of the stock market, you should follow what I call, *The Five Key Principles of Investing*:

Principle #1—Buy Quality

Stocks go up when company profits go up. There is a strong correlation between what the market does and what companies earn. Warren

Buffet, chairman of Berkshire Hathaway, and perhaps the most outstanding investor of our times, has made an absolute killing in the stock market by purchasing large blocks of well-known and well-managed industry leaders such as Coca-Cola, Gillette, Geico, and American Express.

There is an immense difference between investing, speculating, and gambling.

Principle #2—Diversify

How many times have we heard the phrase, "Don't put all of your eggs in one basket"? This philosophy is definitely true when it comes to investing. A diversified portfolio can reduce risk by dividing investment dollars among a variety of investments, such as stocks, bonds, money market funds, and real estate. The following illustration shows how diversification can help maximize growth potential while minimizing risk over time:

Investment Results for Investor A and Investor B over a 25 year period of time*

Investor A	Investor B	
$100,000 at 8%	$20,000 at 15% return =	$858,379
	$20,000 at 10% return =	$216,694
	$20,000 at 5% return =	$67,727
	$20,000 at break even =	$20,000
	$20,000 at total loss =	0_____
Totals: $684,850		$962,800

Example for illustrative purposes only. The numbers are hypothetical and not intended to reflect actual investment returns for any product or security.

Principle #3—Buy Systematically

Simply put, systematic investing means making regular investments at set intervals over time. This disciplined approach allows you to focus on long-term financial goals and not on the short-term ups and downs of the market.

Until the beginner investor perfects the investment process, they should use a professional financial advisor—preferably someone who has been in the business at least 5-10 years.

When you invest systematically, you buy more shares when prices are low and fewer shares when prices increase. This concept is also called dollar cost averaging.* Investing just $100/month for 30 years into one of the mutual funds established in 1928 would have grown to over $500,000, which is a 14.4% average annual return. Dollar cost averaging can be very effective. *(*Investments must be regular and the same amount each time. If the investor discontinues the plan when the market value is less than the cost of the shares, he or she will lose money. The investor must be willing and able to invest during the low price levels. This plan does not protect the investor in a steady declining market.)*

Principle #4—Use Professional Advice

For many investors, professional advice can make a big difference in the outcome of their investment returns. Going it alone, new investors easily self-destruct because their tendency is to purchase a stock or mutual fund featured in a financial magazine. The problem with this is that by the time the publication gets into the hands of small investors, the investment may have already seen its best days.

The first time investor usually buys high and dumps the investment the first time there is a downturn, thus—selling low. Buying low and selling high obviously works much better. The reality is that the novice investor will look for the hot fund (buying high), instead of looking for something that has been ice cold for the past couple of years (buying low) that may be ready for a turnaround.

An example is buying pharmaceutical stocks after they went down 40-50% in 1992-94. Since then, many drug

Dollar cost averaging:
buying more shares when prices are low, fewer when prices are high.

company stocks have more than tripled. Until the beginner investor perfects the investment process, they should use a professional financial advisor—preferably someone who has been in the business at least 5-10 years. Let the new kid on the block practice on someone else—not you.

Principle #5—Buy for the Long Term

Unless you are nearing the point of withdrawing your fund, it's better to have a long term perspective, at least 3-5 years. Although prolonged bear markets are a possibility, the variability of average annual returns over long periods of time is much less than over shorter periods. Patience helps the investor survive the ups and downs of the stock market.

Sure, the market was up roughly two out of three years since 1990. But what about the down years? The market's 31 down years averaged a negative 13.32% return—but the 67 up years averaged a positive 22.32%. And the market has had back-to-back negative years only once

Unless you are nearing the point of withdrawing your fund, it's better to have a long term perspective, at least 3-5 years.

since World War II. The moral of the story? Over time, the positives have out-gained the negatives. So don't look at the bumps in the road—keep an eye on your long-term goals.

When asked the secret to investing in the stock market, Peter Lynch, one of the greatest mutual fund managers, responded—"not to get scared out of the market."

John Templeton, also one of the great portfolio managers of the past 50 years, is often asked what the secret is to successful investing strategies. His answer—"Ignore fluctuations. Do not try to outguess the stock market. Buy a quality portfolio and invest for the long term."

> "Ignore fluctuations. Do not try to outguess the stock market. Buy a quality portfolio and invest for the long term."
>
> —Sir John Templeton

A recent Morningstar study showed that the average annual return for 199 no-load growth funds was 12% from 1984 to 1994, but the average investor earned just 2% over that period. Why? Because much of the time they were out of the market.

Don't get left behind; get started today. Because, after all, money doesn't take care of itself.

(R. Richard Everett, Registered Financial Consultant (RFC), is the founder and president of the Everett Financial Group, Inc. He has spent sixteen years in the financial services industry, including six years as Senior VP for one of the nation's largest financial services companies. Richard and his wife live in Connecticut with their two children.)

18

I'm Investing, Now What?

Top ten common sense tips for asset management.

by Scott Fehrenbacher

After spending nearly two decades in the financial services business from starting as a stockbroker trained by E.F. Hutton in New York to being a part of the online financial revolution today, I have found that the best question I have ever been asked by a customer seeking advice was, "Knowing what you know, what would you do if you were me?"

The good news is that there are nearly an unlimited number of ways and strategies to be successful in investing and managing your money. The bad news is that there is an unlimited number of people, businesses, advertisements, magazines, radio experts, and television shows all ready to tell you what they think you should do.

The question to ask: "Knowing what you know, what would you do if you were me?"

Don't despair. Among the many successful ways are some common denominators that all seem to revolve around common sense. Even the Bible adds some invaluable advice: "The person who strays from common sense will end up in the company of the dead" (Proverbs 21:16).

In response to "What would I do if I were you," here are my top ten common sense tips for asset management:

Tip #1. Don't fall in love with a stock

On dozens of occasions I have had customers who treat stock like their own children. The thought of selling any of their stock in a certain company seemed to be the equivalent of asking them to sacrifice a child. Don't let emotions get involved with your stock. Even if you are holding stock that your parents passed on to you that has great sentimental meaning, you must remember that it represents a commodity of value only.

Don't let emotions get involved with your stock.

I once worked with a widow who owned hundreds of thousands of dollars of interest-rate sensitive electric utility stocks. Even in the face of severe drops in market value as interest rates rose, she refused to reduce the amount of declining stock she had because it was her late-husband who purchased it. Her feelings ended up costing her over one hundred thousand dollars.

Tip #2. Don't buy or sell from a broker on the last two days of a calendar month

If you do not know your financial advisor well, and he or she is paid based on commission, put a moratorium on any business during the last few days of any month. This is typically when commission-based brokers end their production period that determines their paycheck for the following month. There is no need to even risk getting recommendations based more on your advisor's need to earn a commission than your need to make money.

Tip #3. Seek a financial advisor through friends or your company's benefits office

Looking for a broker?
If your friends can't recommend one, utilize the due diligence that your company's benefits office has done on the company's behalf and ask them for a referral.

Brokerage companies often have rookie brokers simply take turns accepting unsolicited calls for advice. One of my friends in San Francisco even got a multi-million dollar account from a famous pro football coach who called him out of the blue. This is far too risky. You wouldn't want to go into brain surgery with a rookie doctor.

You should protect your money, too. If your friends can't recommend one, utilize the due diligence that your company's benefits office has done on the company's behalf and ask them for a referral.

Tip #4. Don't pay for advice you don't need

There will always be a need for high quality full-service stockbrokers. However, the Internet has opened the doors of Wall Street to the common investor like never before. Cost savings are enormous and personal control is greatly improved if you can invest a few hours per week into the powerful research tools and portfolio management applications afforded by free Internet sites.

The Internet has opened the doors of Wall Street to the common investor.

Tip #5. Fee-based managers can gouge, too

If you have avoided commission-based advisors and are paying a professional manager a flat fee based on the size of your portfolio, you need to make sure that you are not paying ongoing management fees of the *cash* portion of your account. It makes sense to pay management fees on the portion of your portfolio that is in stocks and bonds, but never accept to pay additional management fees on the portion of your portfolio invested in money market funds.

Tip #6. Take the best of both worlds

If you have a complex portfolio and estate, consider paying a professional financial advisor for a specific plan that can be executed and evaluated on your own at a discount or online broker. This keeps you in control and free to measure performance without any conflict of interest as well as saving significantly on needless fees and commissions.

Do your research, get outside advice if necessary, and find a core strategy that you can live with long-term.

Tip #7. That's my plan and I'm sticking to it

Too many investors change their core strategy with every new cover of *Money Magazine*. Do your research, get outside advice if necessary, and find a core strategy that you can live with long-term. It is the fees, tax liability, and needless short-term losses that can destroy the multiplying momentum of your portfolio over time if you allow yourself to be whipsawed with every new fad.

Ten tips for asset management

1. Don't fall in love with a stock
2. Don't buy or sell from a broker on the last two days of a calendar month
3. Seek a financial advisor through friends or your company's benefits office
4. Don't pay for advice you don't need
5. Fee-based managers can gouge, too
6. Take the best of both worlds
7. That's my plan and I'm sticking to it
8. Life insurance is not an investment Investments are not life insurance
9. Don't overlook invisible losses
10. Keep your perspective

Tip #8. Life insurance is not an investment. Investments are not life insurance

I can't count the number of insurance salespersons I have met who said life insurance could be used as effective investments. No surprise that none of them had a license to sell anything but insurance. Conversely, stockbrokers without an insurance license may try to convince you that your life insurance premiums are better spent by investing in their investment recommendations. Common sense and good advice will tell you that there is a need for both at some level in every family. Don't let a salesperson convince you of what doesn't make sense.

Tip #9. Don't overlook invisible losses

Invisible losses are those you are taking and not even knowing it. For example, if you are so frightened of accepting some reasonable risk in your investments to your own personally appropriate degree that you would rather place your money in a bank savings account, you will have invisible losses. Had you invested with some common-sense risk, you could have earned a great deal more than you did. This is the definition of risk, because you did lose money. You just don't recognize it. Manage your money, and consider the cost of doing nothing when you make financial decisions.

Tip #10. Keep your perspective

One of my wealthiest clients had a great deal of money in bonds, stocks, and cash. With millions of dollars that you might think would buy personal and emotional freedom, it ended up having the exact opposite effect on him.

Always remember where your portfolio ranks in your own personal priorities of life.

He constantly worried about his money and his responsibility to manage it. He was so frugal that he lived in a mobile home and drove a fifteen year old car. He would spend days reconciling his annual trading logs at the end of the year to make sure that my firm's statements agreed with his own personal calculations to the penny. Unfortunately, the money owned him more than he owned his money.

Always remember where your portfolio ranks in your own personal priorities of life.

Extra Tip #11. Hot tips.

This is simple. **Don't** *buy or sell on hot tips.*

Above all, use your common sense. Take advantage of today's unprecedented access to financial news, research, and tools. And always remember to count your blessings.

(Scott Fehrenbacher spent nearly fourteen years as a financial advisor, then founded the Institute for American Values Investing in Seattle, Washington (featured nationwide from CNBC to the New York Times and Money Magazine). Today he manages the personal finance, business, and careers channels for Washington, D.C.-based Crosswalk.com, the nation's largest Christian Internet portal site.)

19

Aligning Your Investments With Your Values

Mutual funds can be as attractive to your conscience as they are to your pocketbook.

by Patrick Johnson

Social conservatives and individuals of faith are waking up to strategies that promote both morally and fiscally sound investing.

James Tremont, an elder in his church, was on his knees at a recent Promise Keepers rally, praying for revival in his country. At the same time, unbeknownst to him, he was actively profiting from the abortion and pornography industry through his retirement plan with a mutual fund investment company.

The growth of mutual funds

Mutual funds are a part of the typical American's every day life. Names like Fidelity and Vanguard have replaced Chevrolet and IBM as public institutions. Over 50% of American households own mutual funds either as a direct investment or through a retirement plan, including IRAs.

The explosive growth of mutual funds has been astounding. There are currently over 10,000 funds in the marketplace with over $5 trillion in assets. The pace is frantic, and the technology mind-boggling behind this phenomenon.

The mutual fund industry is one of the major suppliers of capital to America's corporations. Peter Drucker, one of

> *The most important source of capital is the average mutual fund transaction of $10,000."*
> —Peter Drucker

the most well respected management gurus in American history, commented on this fact in a 1997 interview in *Forbes* magazine: "The combined sources of money from retail investors, pension funds, and retirement plans are the fastest-growing source of money (to the world economy). The most important source of capital is the average mutual fund transaction of $10,000."

This leads to an interesting question: "What types of companies are your dollars funding through your mutual fund?" If you know the answer to this question, you are in the minority. A recent poll showed that 66 percent of Americans could not list even one stock in their mutual fund portfolio. Many people are unknowingly investing in mutual funds whose holdings run counter to their convictions.

What types of companies are your dollars funding through your mutual fund?

Where's your investment?

When individuals invests their money in a mutual fund, it is combined with billions of other dollars invested by thousands of other shareholders. The mutual fund portfolio manager then uses this large pool of money to make stock purchases on behalf of the fund and the fund shareholders. And the majority of portfolio managers only look at the financial considerations of the stocks they purchase; they do not take into account the social activities of these companies.

Matt Fredericks, a seminary graduate and Christian talk show host, discovered the real life application of this concept in his own investments recently. Matt is passionate about his religious beliefs and seeks to incorporate these principles into every area of his life. This can be seen in his relationship to his children and wife, his outspoken views expressed through his radio program, and his involvement in church and other ministries. However, when Matt sat down with his financial advisor to review his retirement portfolio, he discovered that over 20% of his mutual fund holdings were invested in corporations involved in such industries as pornography and abortion. He was outraged that he was profiting from the very industries that he often fought against in the public eye.

Matt found that 20% of his mutual fund holdings were invested in corporations he did not agree with.

Socially Responsible Investing

It was this inconsistency that initiated a movement over 25 years ago called Socially Responsible Investing (SRI). The idea originated in the church as a means of encouraging parishioners to divest their money from industries deemed to support South-African apartheid. Along the way, other groups found ways to screen for funds and stocks that supported the tobacco and alcohol industries.

New investment companies... are creating mutual funds and other tools to assist investors in aligning investments with beliefs.

Today, over $1 trillion in assets is managed using a Socially Responsible Investing methodology. But while the movement began as an effort to promote laudable causes, it has drifted since into an array of left-of-center issues including screening for investments in companies involved in nuclear power production, the manufacture of firearms, and a host of environmental concerns.

Using issues such as these as their foundation, SRI mutual funds have nearly doubled their money under management between 1995-1997 and the movement is picking up steam.

In this booming investment movement, a void is becoming more and more apparent. Millions of socially conservative investors feel their concerns are being largely ignored when it comes to developing socially responsible screening criteria. In an effort to fill this void, new investment companies, owned by those who hold a conservative worldview, are creating mutual funds and other tools to assist these investors in aligning investments with beliefs.

Sir John Templeton

Sir John Templeton, one of the most successful money managers in modern times and founder of the Templeton funds, has long been a proponent in ethical investing. He sums it up nicely when he said, "You wouldn't want to be the owner of a company that is producing harm for the public, and therefore, you wouldn't want to be the owner of a share of a company that's producing harm for the public."

And Sir John did not simply speak this quote as a nice sounding philosophy to impress others, he put it into practice. His funds have always taken into account this principle when deciding which companies to invest in on behalf of their shareholders. And the Templeton Foreign Fund has been a leader in international investing with one of the most impressive long-term track records in the industry, all while following an ethical investing philosophy.

Your $10,000 mutual fund investment, combined with all of the other $10,000 mutual fund investments, is a powerful source of fuel for corporations in today's economy.

What Sir John understood is that ethical investing is one important component of a consistent stewardship philosophy. Most individuals realize that life is simply a short journey. Because of this, to accumulate wealth simply for the sake of accumulation is foolish. You should leverage your wealth for the benefit of others. One practical implication of stewardship is to give to organizations that help those who are less fortunate.

Simply giving not enough

But simply giving to these types of quality organizations while investing in companies that harm society through the production of products such as pornography or tobacco is an inconsistent stewardship philosophy. It's like trying to put out a fire with a water hose in one hand, while your other hand is pouring gasoline on the same fire. It simply won't work.

Your $10,000 mutual fund investment, combined with

all of the other $10,000 mutual fund investments, is a powerful source of fuel for corporations in today's economy. If socially conservative investors would individually apply a consistent stewardship philosophy in their personal investments, then the sum total of these individual decisions could play an important role in determining what types of companies get the economic fuel necessary to survive. Under this scenario, those businesses that produce products or services harmful to others would be cut off from the fuel supply, while those who build others up would have more than enough fuel to advance quickly into the new millennium.

Who can help:

- *Values Investment Forum*
- *Shepherd Values Funds*
- *Timothy Plan*
- *Noah Fund*
- *Cornerstone Capital Management*
- *Dean Investment Associates*

Next time you make a contribution to your retirement plan

So consider this the next time you make a contribution to your retirement plan through a payroll deduction. Every contribution is more fuel to the corporations. Make sure your fuel is being utilized according to your own personal convictions.

Money is a powerful force. Use yours to benefit others by both your giving and investing decisions carried out through your personal stewardship philosophy.

Your portfolio and who can help

Values Investment Forum offers a free screening program that screens the portfolio holdings of over 4,000 mutual funds to determine how much of a portfolio consists of companies involved in the abortion, pornography, gambling, tobacco and alcohol industries as well as those companies involved in the promotion of non-marriage lifestyles. You can access this program at (www.shepherdvalues.com).

Shepherd Values Funds (877-636-2766), created by Shepherd Financial Services, has a family of funds designed to exclude companies whose products or activities support the industries mentioned above. These six funds cover all of the major asset categories and are managed by such well-known investment advisory firms as Templeton and Nicholas-Applegate.

Timothy Plan (www.timothyplan.com or 800-846-7526) funds also exclude companies from investment based on conservative religious principals. The funds have recently been expanded to include more asset classes. The Timothy funds, like the Shepherd funds, are distributed through brokers, financial planners and other investment professionals, thereby offering assistance in comparing returns, expense ratios and suitability.

For the do-it-yourself investor, the *Noah Fund* (www.noahfund.com or 800-794-6624) may be an option worth considering. Although the fund utilizes more limited screening criteria than both Shepherd and Timothy, it has an excellent 3-year track record and donates a percentage of the advisory fee to religious organizations.

Finally, if you are an individual or institutional investor with over $100,000 to invest, you can employ *Cornerstone Capital Management* (www.ccmadvisers.com or 800-826-5721) or *Dean Investment Associates* (www.chdean.com or 800-327-3656) to create customized portfolios designed to achieve excellent financial returns while following your specific social policy.

(Patrick Johnson is the President of the Values Investment Forum (VIF), a research organization that provides values-based research on stocks and mutual funds to socially conservative institutions, investment advisors and mutual fund companies. He lives in Tupelo, MS with his wife, Jennifer, and their four children.)

20

How to Spot Trends in the Stock Market

Current technology allows you to understand and predict the market like never before.

by Robb Baldwin

Professional stock market watchers, also called technical analysts, have investment methods that judge when the market is ready to make a major move. Every investor should follow these indicators as they can help determine if you're buying in at the starting point of a rally or toward the finish.

Technical analysis turns supply and demand into a visual format for individuals to study and determine the direction of both individual stocks and the overall market.

These indicators translate into lines on charts that when analyzed can be very useful in helping determine the future of the market. With the help of the Internet, anyone can take advantage of technical analysis that has now become so popular on many different websites.

Why should individual investors learn technical analysis and believe that it works? The answer is as simple as supply and demand. The price of a stock is always being auctioned, with buyers and sellers meeting each other's prices to complete transactions. If there are more buyers in the market than sellers, the stock will rise, and inversely, more sellers in the market than buyers means the stock price will fall. Technical analysis turns supply and demand into a visual format for individuals to study and determine the direction of both individual stocks and the overall market.

The following indicators can be used to help you determine the next trend in the market.

Five indicators to spot trends

1. Momentum

This means the speed with which market averages, such

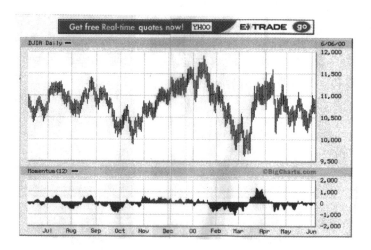

as the NASDAQ stock index, rise or fall. A chart diagramming the price defines whether a stock is rising or falling. However, an oscillator chart tells us the rate at which it is rising or falling or moving up and down.

This type of oscillator tells us whether the trend is gaining or losing momentum. If the index continues rising, but at a slower and slower rate everyday, it may be heading for a fall. However if the speed of the market continues slower as the market moves downward, the market may be bottoming and ready for an upswing.

On a chart, momentum is measured with a line between 0 and 100. When the line is moving upward and crosses 50, this is considered positive. The opposite is true when the line moves downward.

Another measurement of this oscillator is when the line moves too far above or below the midpoint, signifying that the market is considered either overbought or oversold.

2. Trading volume

During a market top scenario, trading volume will display a tendency to be less during rallies than pullbacks. The opposite occurs as the market begins to bottom, and the volume will lighten on pullbacks and be heavy on up days.

In neutral market patterns, volume will typically be light, showing indecision in the marketplace. Heavy volume on either a positive or negative day usually shows a break in this neutral pattern one way or the other.

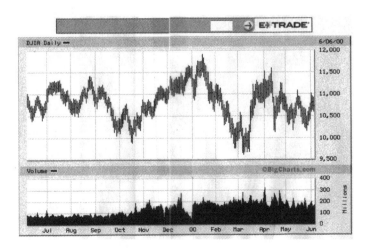

Top five indicators

1. Momentum
2. Trading volume
3. Relative Strength
   Index (RSI)
4. The advance/
   decline line
5. Moving average
   convergence
   divergence (MACD)

3. Relative Strength Index (RSI)

The main reason this mathematical oscillator has become so popular is the upper and lower boundaries that are defined in a range of 0 to 100. Readings over 70 are used to consider overbought, while readings below 30 are to be considered oversold. Just looking at these indicators creates a simple way to determine the market environment based upon the lines generated by the on-balance volume.

For example, if the market rises on volume of 1 billion shares one day only to fall the next day on 500 million shares, the on-balance volume is -50. That is a bullish signal. But when the on-balance volume turns down, it could be a signal that the buying power is nearly exhausted and that stock values are about to sag.

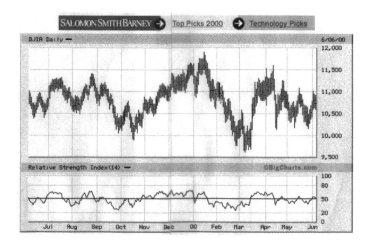

4. Advance/decline line

This simply is a daily count of the number of stocks that rise and the number of stocks that fall. When the gainers outnumber losers, the advance/decline line goes up, which is a sign that the market is getting stronger. When losers outnumber the gainers, the advance/decline line goes down, which tends

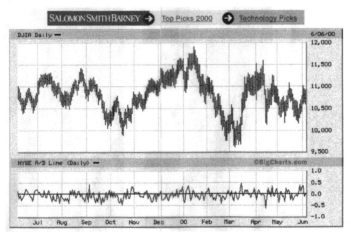

to be a sign of weakness in the market.

Many times you will hear the advance/decline line used to determine the measured *breath* of a stock market advance or decline.

5. Moving Average Convergence Divergence indicator, better known as MACD

This indicator combines the two types of indicators that make up the indicators above (oscillators and moving averages). Because this indicator uses simple math, it is easy to explain.

The indicator is made up of two lines, with the first being the difference between two moving averages of the price over two different periods (usually 12 and 26). The computer subtracts the longer period from the shorter period to obtain this line. The second line is generally one period measure (usually 9).

The result of these two numbers combining themselves on one chart is that the faster moving MACD line will force a crossing over of the slower moving average line, generating either a positive or negative indicator depending on the direction of the MACD line.

If the MACD line is lower than the moving average and crosses over while moving upward, a positive signal is generated. If the MACD line is higher than the moving average line and crosses over while turning  *View your own results —online.* downward, a negative signal is generated. This crossing over is where the name convergence/divergence comes from.

The MACD indicator can also be used with a weekly chart instead of a daily chart. The weekly MACD indicator is a great way to determine the longer-term strength of the market. Because it is based on a longer-term oscillation, it will swing less frequently and avoid false signals.

The final result of learning these indicators is the ability to have a better perspective on how your investment ideas fit into the overall investment spectrum. For many years

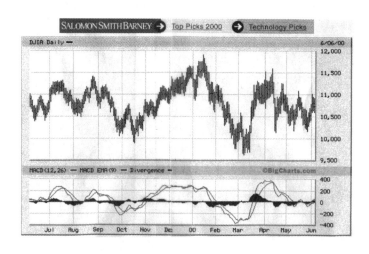

investors have never had these tools available for scrutiny.

Now, however, hundreds of financial websites currently have all of these indicators at your disposal, and you can view them with the click of a mouse. Using them will enable you to see and understand more of what the professional investors use to determine their investments and eliminate any guesswork in the future.

(Robb W. Baldwin, RIA, has been in the financial services business since 1984 and is CEO of Portfolio Management & Research, Inc. and President/CEO of Trade-PMR Discount Brokerage. He manages individual and institutional money for both qualified and non-qualified accounts.)

VI

Making Money
— You Can Start
Your Own Business

21

Money Is Only an Idea

Everything you need—to take you anywhere you want to go—is right between your ears.

by Paul J. Meyer

"Am I going to have to do manual labor all my life?" I remember asking my mother this heartfelt question shortly after my fifteenth birthday. The wisdom of her response profoundly influenced the direction of my life. She put her hands on my head—one on each side—and, looking me straight in the eyes, she said, "You have everything you need right here between your ears. In your head, you have everything you will ever need to take you anywhere you want to go, to have anything you want to have, and to be anything you want to be."

I believed her. At that moment I knew the world's abundance was mine, to earn and to possess. I could choose to remain a migrant fruit picker, or I could stake my claim on the world's resources and riches. The choice was mine, and everything depended on my attitude.

In your head, you have everything you will ever need to take you anywhere you want to go, to have anything you want to have, and to be anything you want to be."

Attitude determines success

Over the years I have realized even more fully the powerful role attitude plays in determining success, including financial success. When people think of themselves as successful, they succeed. When they think of themselves as wealthy, they usually do what it takes to become wealthy. In contrast, people who *feel* inferior *act* inferior.

A poor self-image is an imposing, impenetrable barrier to achieving financial success.

People who consider themselves failures fail. People who think of themselves as poor remain poor. A poor self-image is an imposing, impenetrable, barrier to achieving financial success.

I have chosen to think of myself as a success.

Attitude toward money determines financial success

Attitude toward money itself also determines financial success. What I think about the nature of money is equally as forceful as what I think about myself and my potential for making money. My belief that money is only an idea, along with my positive self-image, is responsible for my success in earning money, saving money, and investing money—and in accumulating assets.

Money itself has no intrinsic value. It is simply printed paper or minted metal worth no more than other paper or metal of comparable size and quality. The difference is in money's exchange value.

Authority and power have historically been vested in ownership of tangible goods. The person with the most tangible goods has always had an advantage because such goods may be traded for other assets—labor, raw materials, or additional goods. Since tangible wealth is cumbersome and in some cases absolutely immobile. Money serves as a substitute—a token that represents valuable possessions.

The paper currency now in circulation consists merely of promissory notes guaranteed by the government. The value of money lies in what others believe it is worth. Its value is based on belief and trust. In this context, money is only an idea. Understanding this concept has been vitally important to my desire and ability to attain financial success.

Most people respect money

A person of wealth once explained that even money has to earn our respect: "Anyone who doesn't spend time working is a disgrace, and money that is not working is even more disgraceful; it doesn't even have any aches and pains to excuse it."

Sharing this pragmatic attitude toward money, few wealthy people have a lot of cash because it is invested. It is busy working for them, making more money. For people with wealth, money and its buying power hold no great sense of awe. It is money's investment power, the power to multiply itself, that commands the interest and attention of those who own it. As a result, most of the world's money is invested in assets other than cash. Most business transactions go on through credit. The credit card is rapidly replacing currency for the average consumer. Plastic money is neither tangible nor concrete; it is merely a concept, an idea.

*Few **wealthy people** have a lot of cash because it is invested. It is busy working for them, making more money.*

Less money in circulation than used in business each day

Numerous other financial facts demonstrate the fact that money is only an idea. For example, there is never as much money in circulation as is transacted in business in a day.

Suppose, for instance, I take a client to lunch and pay the restaurant fifty dollars. The restaurant owner uses the fifty dollars to pay a supplier for fresh vegetables and other foods. The supplier, in turn, uses the fifty dollars to pay a truck driver who delivers the food. The driver then buys food and clothing. Transactions totaling two hundred dollars take place rapidly using only the original fifty dollars.

This illustration makes two points: first, the importance of cash is highly exaggerated, and second, money is only an idea.

Value of money varies

Another related idea about money is that its value varies and depends upon *what* is bought, *when* and *where*. A twenty dollar bill does not, of course, mysteriously change into a fifty or a hundred, but its value varies. In the hands of a foolish or extravagant spendthrift, a twenty dollar bill might purchase only five dollars' worth of goods. At a different time, in the hands of a discerning person, the twenty dollars might be used wisely to buy goods that can become worth fifty dollars.

The Bible itself says that "wealth certainly makes itself wings" (*Proverbs 23:5*). Enjoying enduring wealth requires a watchful eye on purchases and investments because money is only as valuable as choices make it.

Enjoying enduring wealth requires a watchful eye on purchases and investments because money is only as valuable as choices make it.

A familiar example of money's fluctuating value is merchants' willingness to sacrifice some profit through reduced prices. Willingness to alter the value they place on their inventory is influenced by their need to secure cash, to pay taxes, to get rid of existing inventory to make room for new items, or various reasons. At such times, the consumers' dollar is worth more, but when shortages of some vital product cause prices to rise, the consumers' dollar purchases less.

While the impulse buyer is not likely to become financially independent, I have learned by experience that neither is the overly cautious.

Variables to consider for financial success

The fluctuating value of money is only one of many variables I take into consideration when planning for my financial success. While the impulse buyer is not likely to become financially independent, I have learned by experience that neither is the overly cautious.

Those who genuinely know money—with all its characteristic merits and foibles—and use it with judgment and daring, gain the prize of financial success. These insightful individuals literally spend their way to wealth as they wisely invest and acquire assets that appreciate in value, such as securities, real property, and equities. To those who understand money, these are just some of the ideas that money represents.

You have everything you need for financial success

When people ask me how they, too, might enjoy the same financial success I have earned, I can almost feel my mother's hands on my head as her words echo in my memory: "You have everything you need right here between your ears."

First of all, I tell them, believe that you have unlimited potential for financial success and growth.

Second, recognize that you are personally responsible for your financial achievements.

Third, develop an attitude and belief that money is only an idea.

(Paul J. Meyer virtually started the self-improvement industry, founding Success Motivation Institute, Inc. in 1960. He has authored twenty-three major programs in personal achievement and leadership training with sales approaching $2 billion worldwide. Paul has five children; he and his wife, Jane, live in Waco, Texas.)

Excerpted with permission from *I Inherited a Fortune*, by Paul J. Meyer, The Summit Publishing Group, 1997

22

The Right
(Entrepreneurial) Stuff

Having what it takes to start a new business is everything.

by A. L. Andrews

Getting started on the right path with the right stuff will greatly enhance the prospect of good results for your business endeavor. Approximately half of the start-up businesses fail each year. Surveys indicate that there are striking similarities with most businesses that fail. In fact, there are only a handful of reasons that account for why many businesses don't make it. Among these are: inadequate capital and cash flow, inadequate planning, and inadequate management skills.

The potential influence of each of these on the success of your venture must be appraised ahead of time. Then resolutions and plans can be made to help you avoid disaster. Knowledge is key to being able to discern potential hazards. Without it, you will be like a pilot flying in a storm with no instruments. You can only judge the situation by how

Approximately half of the start-up businesses fail each year.

Three reasons businesses fail:
1—inadequate capital and cash flow,
2—inadequate planning,
3—inadequate management skills

current conditions feel. This kind of input is usually not totally reliable and often comes too late. Making sure that you have all the facts up front is the only way you can be confident that you are doing everything you can to provide a reasonable expectation of making it.

Five steps to getting prepared

Regardless of the challenges you may face in starting your business, you can deal with them more easily and with greater confidence if you prepare yourself. Prepare yourself beforehand. Firmly establishing what assets you have, what you will need to get the job done, where you want to go, and the guidelines and principles that you will apply to keep you on track.

1. Set priorities in order

• **First,** seek God continually.

• **Second,** do not neglect the relationship responsibility with your spouse and children, and keep the communications working.

• **Third,** your business.

If any of this is out of order, it will not matter how hard you work, failure is just around the corner. Your business goals and objectives are only valid after all else is in order.

2. Get advice.

Talk with others who have started businesses, especially

ones like you are entering into. Use the services of good professionals in resolving complex, technical, or legal concerns. Businesses, like people, are destroyed for lack of knowledge.

3. Assess your business-related strengths and weaknesses.

Properly assess yourself, then spend most of your effort perfecting and applying your strengths. Do not spend too much time on your weaknesses, as this can become a major distraction. Consider how you can utilize other resources to fill-in for areas where you are short on experience, education, etc.

4. Write a meaningful business plan.

Take the time to write a good business plan, since this will not only help you establish greater confidence in what you are doing, but it will also help you make more informed decisions and avoid potential pitfalls.

5. Have fun.

This does not mean we always go around laughing (but that's not a bad idea). We can determine how we are going to respond to any situation and, in the strength of the Lord (*Philippians 4:13*), press on in faith, peace, and joy. If you stop having fun, stop and find out what is not being handled correctly.

> Though it is not always possible to have specific plans for each event before it has appeared, it is possible to brace for the hidden demands of entrepreneurship.

Those starting a business, especially if it is the first one, will find themselves facing a new set of demands. Demands that they may have *never* encountered before. They must brace themselves for this whole new assortment of circumstances, challenges, and obstacles. The word *brace* is significant and used here with reason.

Though it is not always possible to have specific plans laid-out for each event before it has appeared, it is possible to *brace* for the *hidden demands of entrepreneurship*. Much can be done, however, to prepare for whatever may come along. After all, "The prudent see danger and take refuge, but the simple keep going and suffer for it" (*Proverbs 27:12*).

Bracing goes beyond just securing good footing and finding something to hang on to. Bracing means to provide support for something. You must build a structure on bedrock that is designed to withstand the onslaught of the enemy, and whatever the private enterprise system can throw against it. The business structure you build must withstand the storms of the business arena, which include interest rates, market conditions, employment, global and national politics, technological changes, and more.

If you desire to keep your own feet firmly planted, you must immerse yourself consistently in the Word of God in order to be ready to take on all the challenges that will come your way. He has much to say on the subject: "Therefore everyone who hears these words of mine and puts them into practice is like a wise man who built his house on the rock. The rain came down, the streams rose, and the winds blew and beat against that house; yet it did not fall, because it had its foundation on the rock" (Matthew 7:24-25).

Running a business can be fulfilling, exciting, and enjoyable, but always remember, the buck will stop with you

If you know for certain that you are called into the business arena, and understand what God's Word says about successful business dealings, it is reasonable to expect success. Part of this is taking an honest look at entrepreneurship and the business you plan to operate. Far too many just jump into a commitment before they consider just what they are really getting into.

You may very well have what it takes to be a successful entrepreneur!

Twelve characteristics of successful business owners

Do you have what it takes to make it as a business owner? Making a realistic assessment of your skills, abilities, and interests should be considered essential. You most likely will not fit the entrepreneur profile exactly, but knowing your strengths and weaknesses gives you an advantage in preparing for the support you may need in running your business.

If your personal profile does not seem to line up with the following profile of characteristics of the typical successful entrepreneur, give some long, hard thought as to whether you are really cut out to be a business owner. The matter of your success is far too important to leave to chance.

1. Drive to achieve

Intelligence, education, experience, appearance, and management skills are all sighted as factors contributing to the success of the entrepreneur. There is one factor, however, that is found most often in highly successful business owners. Such individuals seem to always have a tremendous drive to achieve. This attitude tends to override everything else and seems to have almost everything to do with success.

2. Desire to succeed

Success is desired over and above any wishes to be liked

Twelve characteristics of successful business owners

1. Drive to achieve
2. Desire to succeed
3. Overall tendency to follow through
4. Positive mental attitude
5. Objective approach
6. A respectful attitude toward money
7. Anticipates developments
8. Resourcefulness
9. Stable relationships
10. Effective communications
11. Technical knowledge
12. Understands own skills:
    a. What do you like to do best?
    b. What are your three major skills?
    c. What can you do better than most people?
    d. What describes your management abilities?
    e. Describe how your experience applies to your business.

or to exercise control. Success can be considered to be the constant achievement of worthwhile goals. Exactly what are worthwhile goals is a matter of individual interpretation. Obviously, any measure of success must agree with the Word of God.

3. Overall tendency to follow through

This applies to any personal commitment or the accomplishment of any task. Even when the going gets tough, the entrepreneur is not apt to quit half-way through. In a word, perseverance.

4. Positive mental attitude

Being generally optimistic even in challenging situations is a kind of attitude that generally grows out of being confident in who you are, and understanding your abilities. Knowing who you are in Christ and that you are called to the business arena are major contributors to this.

5. Objective approach

This entails the ability to realistically and accurately view each situation and assess associated risks and determine an appropriate course of action. Being able to honestly determine one's own abilities and limitations is vital, as is not thinking more highly of yourself than you ought.

6. A respectful attitude toward money

This includes a tendency to look upon money as a means for accomplishing things, rather than as a thing to be sought after as an end in itself. The love of money is still the root of all evil.

7. A tendency to anticipate developments

Those who possess the ability to see things coming are able to take the appropriate course of action, rather than reacting only when circumstances are upon them. The prudent see danger and protect themselves.

8. Resourcefulness

The ability to solve unique problems in unique ways is vital for entrepreneurs. They are often demanded to handle new developments with no previous experience to rely on as a guide.

9. Stable relationships

Being emotionally stable, cheerful, cooperative, and able to get along well with employees and associates are vitally important characteristics of successful business owners.

10. Effective communications

The ability to effectively communicate and present your ideas by both verbal and written means is extremely important. You must be able to communicate an idea or vision beyond just stating the facts in order to generate a response in others.

11. Technical knowledge

An entrepreneur is usually well-rounded, knowledgeable about business operations and practices, and able to effectively utilize information towards effecting reasonable results.

12. Understands own skills

If you have never taken an aptitude or skills assessment tests, I recommend it. Successful entrepreneurs have taken a good, honest look at themselves. The tests are designed to get you thinking,, not provide any hard fixed assessments or answers about your skills, and it is up to you whether you take the tests or not. Describing in detail the following five questions would be a good place to start:

Five basics for success in business

1. Be knowledgeable
2. Have something to offer
3. Be willing to work
4. Be committed to excellence
5. Believe the Word of God

a. What do you like to do best?

b. What are your three major skills?

c. What can you do better than most people?

d. Describe your management abilities.

e. Describe how your experience applies to your business.

The next step

Running a business is nothing like working for someone else. You are responsible for everything. Truly, the buck stops with you. Are you a self-starter, capable of planning, organizing, and carrying out projects on your own initiative? If not, you may find starting and running a business a miserable existence. If this all still sounds good to you, operating your own business can be a source of immense satisfaction, and can provide many wonderful rewards.

Once you have taken a good look at what you are made of and found out if you have some of the *right stuff,* there are still many steps that go into having a successful business.

Finding out all that you need to know about your business should consume you from this point on. This includes gathering all the information you can and placing all this data in an organized package that will make up your business plan. The final product makes up your set of charts you will need to keep your business on course towards success. It will never be static, but always subject to adjustments. It provides you with an indication of the resources that will be needed and an important bench mark to measure your progress by.

After all, it's your business and your future.

Five basics for success in business

Success and profit are a by-product of attending to certain basics. If you focus on the proper elements and diligently pursue maximum effect, success and profit should follow. But, no matter how gifted you may be, if you neglect the basics, performance will always suffer.

1. Be knowledgeable

Someone once said, "Never invest in something you don't know a lot about." How true this is. If you are planning on operating your own business, your number one job must be finding out all you can about the business. Failure to invest the time to discover what it takes to operate a business effectively could be disastrous. The more knowledge you gain, the greater your prospects for success.

Never invest in something you know nothing about.

2. Have something to offer

You cannot help but succeed if you are looking for ways to meet the needs of the customer. Just because you and your family and friends think your idea is great, doesn't mean you have something to offer to a broad prospective customer base. Remember, the customers will not think like you do. A good business idea is only good if someone else is willing to spend money on it.

3. Be willing to work

Looking for an easy way to make a living? Operating your own business is not it. Chasing get-rich-quick schemes will lead to poverty, not prosperity. Success takes commitment to a long-term endeavor requiring diligence and, most of the time, hard work.

4. Be committed to excellence

It is not enough to do only what is necessary. Your customers and potential customers need to see a consistent quality in your business. You should purpose to be superior, going above and beyond anything the competition offers. Excellence takes effort and commitment, but neglecting excellence will slowly (sometimes not so slowly) cause business to decline.

5. Believe the Word of God

The most important basic to business success is settling in your heart that God's Word is relevant for today's business issues. When the prevailing wisdom of business does not line up with the Word, you must be ready to accept and implement the biblical principles over the world's approach. Know these principles about conducting your business affairs, then be diligent to consistently apply them.

Excellence takes effort and commitment.

(A.L. Andrews, an independent business consultant since 1989, specializes in the areas of finance, planning, computer applications, and management & leadership training for small businesses. He has 22 years of banking and corporate finance experience and is a graduate of California State Polytechnic University in Pomona, California.)

23

Full of Potential

Potential is unlimited, but like a pocket in a new suit, we may need to locate and un-stitch what inhibits us.

by Ken Wallace

When you purchase a new suit or jacket, the pockets are usually sewed up and must be clipped in order to get into them. Even so, without a proper philosophy of money and wealth, you will not attract or hold anything in your pockets because they are still sewed shut. A proper view of finances will open your pockets to receive the abundance of life intended for you.

A lesson from the future

In the television series, "Star Trek: The Next Generation," twenty-third century human beings have eliminated the need and desire for money. This has helped them transcend their roots on Earth and take wing to the stars and other planets. However, even though humans have overcome the need and desire for money, there exists an alien race of

Without a proper philosophy of money and wealth, you will not attract or hold anything in your pockets because they are still sewed shut.

mercenary merchants whose sole purpose for existence is to amass interstellar currency, and whose sole measure of personal worth is the amount of their personal wealth.

Gene Roddenbury, the creator of Star Trek, was an astute analyst of the human civilization of the 20th century. In his futuristic alien race obsessed with and blinded by money, he saw a present-day parallel in societies all across planet Earth. These beings serve to teach the lesson that money is not a sound or solid basis for human endeavor or relationship. When money is the primary end that is sought through the energies of life, it soon becomes the means for measuring the value of those energies, and of life itself.

> When money is the primary end that is sought through the energies of life, it soon becomes the means for measuring the value of those energies, and of life itself.

When this happens, life actually becomes impoverished because it no longer is seen to have dimension or possibilities or worth beyond the profit line. Life is viewed as the ability, or inability, to accumulate wealth in order to secure worth. The absurdity and poverty of such an understanding of life is well summarized in the words of a bumper sticker I saw recently: "The one who dies with the most stuff wins." I wonder what the prize will be.

Civilized life without money

Roddenbury appears to be asking the question, "What would civilized life be like without money?" Would it be some cosmic communist collective devoted to share and share alike? Where would the resources come from to support and sustain every human life? How would such resources be fairly allocated and distributed so that the ones with the greatest need would receive the greatest share? Would these resources be of sufficient quality to enable people to grow and expand their personal attributes and natural abilities? Would there be enough to go around?

Roddenbury answers these questions by introducing a machine called the "replicator," a ubiquitous device that creates whatever one desires, literally out of thin air. All required resources for living and growing could be summoned at the moment they were needed or desired in the necessary quantities with no waste or want. Of course this is pure fantasy. However, there is more to this story.

With the replicator, Roddenbury was able to divorce resource development, acquisition, and distribution from all work activities. Twenty-third century human beings didn't have to work in order to obtain the resources necessary to sustain and develop life. These celestial citizens worked for the pleasure of self-expression and to apply their talents and energies to making ever-increasing contributions to the greater good of human civilization. Work was an end in itself and not a means to obtain money in order to secure resources necessary for survival and development.

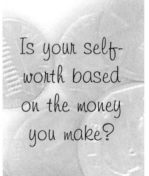

Is your self-worth based on the money you make?

Separating money and work

By separating work and money, work became wealth because it no longer needed to be performed for money. Wealth and money were severed from each other for good. Instead of money, what one did to contribute to the greater good, and to the accomplishment of the collective mission, was the measure of personal wealth and worth.

I think we 21st century beings can learn a valuable lesson from the Star Trek generation of the future when it comes to how best to manage money and the resources it buys. If we could learn to view work as an end in itself, and not merely as a means to obtain money, then the experiences of our work would become the wealth we acquire regardless of the amount of money it produces. The issue here is that work builds character, good work builds good character, and good character is true wealth. Work, then, becomes the means for wealth not by what we get for it (money), but by what we become by it (character).

Good character produces a wealth of happiness, healthfulness, and personal fulfillment that money cannot buy. There are many things money can buy and just as many it can't. Money can buy a house but not a home, a bed but not a good night's sleep. Those things it cannot buy must be attracted into one's life by good character. Otherwise, they will remain elusive and, without them, life becomes impoverished even in the midst of monetary wealth.

> Money can buy a house but not a home, a bed but not a good night's sleep.

Now that we've established a proper view of work, money, and wealth, we need to examine the means of fleshing out such a philosophy. What does it take to actually practice building a wealthy character? In a word, it takes discipline.

Discipline and regret

Aside from physical pain, there are really only two other types of pain that human beings experience. Both are more psychic than physical, although, in both cases, there can be unpleasant physical manifestations. One is the pain of discipline, the other is the pain of regret. The latter occurs as a consequence of the absence of the former.

Pain of discipline

Author and columnist, (the late) Erma Bombeck, once commented that the trouble with life is that it's so daily. Likewise, discipline is a daily decision. As anyone who resolves to lose some weight or get into shape soon discovers, getting from deciding to do to actually doing can involve a tremendous amount of agonizing effort.

Once the implementation of the resolution occurs, the changed behavior results in pain because new behaviors must replace the old ones. Neurological research has indicated that when a person changes a fundamental belief or opinion which, in turn, determines behavior, the brain undergoes a series of nervous sensations equivalent to distressing torture. It is when this distress is fully felt that the attempts at changing behavior often fade into forgetfulness.

Creatures of Habit:

Neurological research has indicated that when a person changes a fundamental belief or opinion which, in turn, determines behavior, the brain undergoes a series of nervous sensations equivalent to distressing torture.

Our natural desire is for comfort and predictability, not challenge and change. Aristotle recognized the courage and difficulty of self-discipline when he said: "I count him braver who overcomes his desires than him who conquers his enemies, for the hardest victory is over self."

"The things you do that you don't have to will always determine who you are when it's too late to do anything about it."
—Hersell Wilson, an early 20th century social commentator

Discipline can also be painful in that it is a process that involves giving up in order to go up. It is disconcerting to give up something of immediate desire in order to obtain something of value later. After all, there is always the risk that you won't actually get the things for which you've sacrificed. But sacrifice is a required element of the equation that opens the pockets and attracts the wealth of life into them.

Pain of regret

As both a businessman and a pastor, I've heard countless people remorsefully utter the following phrases: "If only I had...", "I wish I had...", and "I should have...". These are words that express deep, soulful pain. When spoken, they proclaim the stark realization that life could have been better than it is now. They are blatant admissions that life is the way it is because of personal choices made and actions done or left undone. This pain of regret can endure throughout a lifetime, and often causes the rest of one's life to descend into bitterness and despair.

Hersell Wilson, an early 20th century social commentator, said: "The things you do that you don't have to will always determine who you are when it's too late to do anything about it."

None of us have to exercise discipline in any aspect of our lives. We are certainly free to choose to do nothing to make something of our lives—to wind up being a nobody by not helping anybody, including ourselves. Self-discipline is voluntary. But there is a heavy price to pay when discipline is not chosen in the area of finances. When it's too late to earn the necessary money to pay the bills, the bills will arrive.

192

When it's too late to save enough for retirement, retirement cannot be taken.

The pain of regret is enormous in comparison to the pain of self-discipline. If your pockets are bare, check to see if the way you view money and wealth is actually keeping them sewed shut.

Two steps to God's abundance

We are creatures fashioned in the image of God. To accurately reflect God in our lives, we need to yield to His desire for us. Whenever we submit ourselves to God's desire for our lives, we broaden and deepen our character as spiritual beings and thereby become capable of receiving spiritual abundance, which includes all wealth.

> *The pain of regret is enormous in comparison to the pain of self-discipline.*

The act of submission is in choosing to do what God does in relation to creation. What God does in relation to creation is to give Himself. We develop a good character by giving ourselves to others. It is this good character, developed in spiritual obedience to God's desire for us, that attracts all manner of wealth into our lives so that we might be optimally equipped to serve others.

When we give ourselves to others, we are actually fulfilling our purpose as the *crown of creation*. We cannot receive until we give. Perhaps it is best put by part of the famous prayer attributed to St. Francis of Assisi:

> *O, Divine Master, grant that I may not so much seek to be consoled as to console; to be understood as to understand; to be loved as to love; For it is in giving that we receive; it is in pardoning that we are pardoned; it is in dying that we are born again to eternal life.*

What do you need to do to broaden and deepen your spiritual character so as to attract more of the abundance of God's wealth into your life? There are just two steps to take.

Step one

Tell God that you submit to His desire for you. Do this every morning. This is the primary act of giving yourself first to God so that God can give Himself again to creation through you. From this moment on you will receive God's abundance so that you can give to others. Whatever you give to others is a sacrifice of praise to the presence of God's abundant life within you.

The irony is that you can't give to others unless you receive from God, and in order to receive from God you must give yourself to God.

When Jesus was asked what the greatest commandment was, He immediately replied, "you shall love the Lord your God with all your heart, and with all your soul, and with all your mind, and with all your strength. The second is this, 'You shall love your neighbor as yourself.' There is no other commandment greater than these" (Mark 12:29-31).

It is fascinating that Jesus added a second commandment. He was linking love of God with love of others (a neighbor is anyone within loving distance).

What must be kept in mind, however, is that there is an order presented here. The first commandment is to love God with all that one is—and not, incidentally, with all that one has. The second flows from the first. How often do we attempt to serve others without first, knowing if they can benefit from our service; second, if we have what is necessary to help and not hinder them; and third, establishing that God has led us to serve them.

The point is that only when we first give ourselves wholly to God can God show us to whom we can most effectively give ourselves.

Never forget the divine irony: you can't give unless you receive; but, in order to receive you must give. Our understanding of this seeming paradox is this: You can't give to others unless you receive from God; in order to receive from God you must give yourself to God.

Step two

The discipline that will keep attracting God's abundance in your life is to daily give yourself to those whom God leads you to without thought of return or reward. Remember the words of Dr. Albert Schweitzer: "Do something for somebody every day for which you do not get paid."

When you take these two simple steps on a daily basis, you'll find your pockets are full of God's richness, and that your true wealth will be a good character that not only survives in this life, but will be filled with the abundance of God's eternal life.

What is inhibiting wealth from coming into *your* life?

An enemy I had, whose face I
    stoutly strove to know,
For hard he dogged my steps unseen
    wherever I did go.
My plans he balked, my aims he foiled,
    he blocked my onward way;
When for some lofty goal I toiled, he
    grimly said to me, "Nay!"
One night I seized and held him fast,
    from him the veil did draw.
I gazed upon his face at last and, lo,
    myself I saw.

(Ken Wallace, known as "The Business Pastor," is a United Methodist minister and a business consultant. He provides reliable resources, instruction, encouragement, motivation and support for business leaders to help them live balanced lives committed to creating both physical and spiritual wealth for their families, employees, customers, shareholders, communities and nations.)

24

Tribute to the Entrepreneur

Entrepreneurs may make mistakes along with their millions, but if it weren't for them, the world would not be what it is today.

by Burton Folsom, Ph.D.

Without question, entrepreneurs have led the way. From computers to cars and from planes to post-it notes, entrepreneurs have changed (and are changing) the way the world works. As a result, the wealth from such creativeness often goes to the first person who claims to be the creative genius. What has yet to be discovered, invented and changed is limitless.

Entrepreneurs have a way of bouncing back, despite the prevailing winds of opposition.

As we look to the future and what is yet to be done, let us remember two men who have benefited our society in countless ways. The first is Elijah McCoy, the second, Henry Ford.

The Real McCoy

Railroads were one of the greatest inventions of the 19th century. One man who was indispensible in helping the railroads run efficiently and on time was a great black inventor, Elijah McCoy.

McCoy was born in 1843 in Canada, where his parents had fled from Kentucky to escape slavery. In Canada, the McCoys learned that individual freedom and education for work in the marketplace were keys to opening opportunities for blacks.

The Real McCoy

Elijah McCoy

— first patent, age 29
— total patents: 51
— last patent, age 80
— founded Elijah McCoy Manufacturing Company in Detroit to make and sell his inventions.

Upon reaching manhood, Elijah McCoy went to Scotland for training in mechanical engineering. When it came time to apply his industrial skills, the Civil War had ended; blacks were legally free; and McCoy came back to the U.S. He settled in Ypsilanti., Michigan, where he began work for the Michigan Central Railroad.

Despite McCoy's training, he was offered the lowly job of locomotive fireman. He accepted it with a determination to show the railroad that he could accomplish more.

He immediately applied his skills to a major problem: the dangerous overheating of locomotives. Trains had to stop regularly to oil engine parts to reduce friction. If trains stopped infrequently, the overheating could damage parts or start fires. If they stopped too often, freight and passengers would be delayed. McCoy invented a lubricating cup that oiled engine parts as the train was moving. He secured a patent for it in 1872 and steadily improved it over time.

Others tried to imitate McCoy's invention, but he kept ahead of them with his superior engineering skills. His standard of quality was so high that to separate his lubricating cup from cheaper imitations it became known as "the real McCoy," which many believe to be the origin of the famous phrase.

The invention helped the Michigan Central run safer and quicker across the state. It was also put to use in stationary engines and even in steamship engines. The grateful management of the Michigan Central promoted McCoy and honored him as a teacher and innovator for the railroad.

McCoy showed remarkable creative energy during the next fifty years. He received 51 more patents, mostly for lubricating devices. Not even old age dimmed his creative light. When he was 77, he patented an improved airbrake lubricator and when he was 80, he patented a vehicle wheel tire. He founded the Elijah McCoy Manufacturing Company in Detroit in 1920 to make and sell his inventions.

On June 4, 1896, Henry Ford smashed open the brick wall of his rented garage with an ax. He had just started his first gas-powered car and it was too big to fit through the door.

McCoy was from a generation of great black inventors and businessmen. They included Humphrey H. Reynolds, who invented the ventilator screens for Pullman cars, and George Washington Carver, who developed hundreds of marketable products, including many derived from the peanut

Elijah McCoy was one of many blacks to use his freedom after the Civil War to improve the American workplace and show skeptical whites what free, enterprising blacks could accomplish. For people of all races who believe in self-help, Elijah was, and still is, an inspiring example of "the real McCoy."

Henry Ford—The man with a better idea

Anyone strolling by 58 Bagley Street in Detroit, Michigan, in the morning of June 4, 1896, would have seen a strange sight: Henry Ford, ax in hand, smashing open the brick wall of his rented garage. He had just started his first gas-powered car and it was too big to fit through the door. It has been over a hundred years since Ford's achievement, and we ought to pause to remember what he did, and marvel at how it changed the world.

Cars:

"a rich man's toy"
—*Henry Ford*

"the new symbol of wealth's arrogance"
—*Woodrow Wilson*

In 1896, Grover Cleveland was just finishing his second term as president of the United States. The automobile was such a novelty that few people other than a handful of tinkerers had even set foot in one. In 1903, the year the Ford Motor Company went into business, the city of Detroit fixed a speed limit of eight miles per hour for almost a mile around city hall. Convicted speeders paid $100, which was about two months' wages for an average American worker. But the "average American worker" was not driving America's first cars. They were, as Ford observed, "a rich man's toy" or, as Woodrow Wilson claimed, the "new Symbol of wealth's arrogance."

Henry Ford changed all that. He didn't invent either the auto or the mass production scheme he so brilliantly employed to churn out cars by the millions. But he did, in his own words, "build a car for the great multitude." When he built the Model T, he "put America on wheels" and made Michigan the car capital of the world.

Ford was an entrepreneur and, as are most entrepreneurs, a visionary as well. His all-American car had to be "large enough for the family." It had to be "constructed of the best materials by the best men to be hired." And it had to be "so low in price that no man making a good salary (would) be unable to own one."

Ford's ingenuity took the assembly line method of production to new heights of productivity and efficiency, but he shook the industrial world to its foundations with an amazing gamble: he doubled wages and reduced working hours.

When Ford cranked out his first Model Ts in 1909, he was well on his way to fulfilling his vision. Sales that year were a modest 18,000; by 1913, he almost reached 250,000; in 1920, he sold over one million Model Ts. Prices fell as fast as sales rose. The first Model Ts were barely under $1,000 each, but by 1920 Ford had cut the price to a mere $355—roughly $3,500 today. With all of their manufactured steel, vulcanized rubber, and processed plate glass, Model Ts were selling for less than 30 cents a pound—perhaps the best bargain in the industrialized world.

How could Ford repeatedly cut prices and boost quality at the same time? His ingenuity took the assembly line method of production to new heights of productivity and efficiency, but he shook the industrial world to its foundations with an amazing gamble: he doubled wages and reduced working hours. "The payment of five dollars a day for an eight-hour day was one of the

Model Ts in any color, as long as it's black!

finest cost-cutting moves we ever made," Ford wrote in the early 1920s. The five-dollar-a-day wage policy reduced turnover, improved morale, and brought some of the best workers to his plants in Michigan. Ford even hired thousands of handicapped but capable workers, including bedridden patients who happily screwed nuts and bolts together on mini-assembly lines in their rooms.

Henry Ford made the best car at the lowest price and earned a billion dollars. Only when he became complacent with the Model T and refused to innovate did he fall from the top.

To Ford, the issues of minimum wages, maximum working hours, the hiring of workers, and the pace of industrial productivity should be resolved by the market, not the government. "Our help does not come from Washington, but from ourselves," he wrote. "The government is a servant and never should be anything but a servant."

Henry Ford made the best car at the lowest price and earned a billion dollars. Only when he became complacent with the Model T and refused to innovate did he fall from the top. "It is strange," he wrote in 1926, "how, just as soon as an article becomes successful, somebody starts to think that it would be more successful if only it were different. There is a tendency to keep monkeying with styles and to spoil a good thing by changing it." He purportedly once said that customers could have any color of car they wanted, so long as it was black.

That kind of thinking had made history out of the horse and buggy makers. In 1927, it would do the same to the Model T. By then, the new Chevrolet from General Motors had a water-pump cooling system, an oil gauge on the dash, a reliable ignition system, a foot accelerator, and a gas tank in the rear for safety and convenience. And, the new Chevys came in a variety of colors. The era of Ford's dominance was over.

Henry Ford didn't always get it right, but he got it right enough times to rank as one of the greatest business geniuses this country has ever produced. His century-old story is an eternal tribute to the free enterprise system—a system which allowed his talents to blossom right here in the U.S. and to benefit untold millions of people the world over.

(Burton Folsom received his Ph.D. in history from the University of Pittsburgh. He has taught at the University of Pittsburgh, University of Nebraska, Murray State University, Northwood University, and Hillsdale College. He is currently Historian in Residence at the Center for the American Idea in Houston, Texas.)

Used with permission by Mackinac Center for Public Policy and Burton Folsom.

VII

Managing Your Business

25

Bringing Up the Bottom Line Profits

Why strong stakeholder relationships are good for the bottom line.

by Janella Griggs

In many corporate budgets today, a very important component is missing: stakeholder relationships. Some managers discount the stakeholders' importance by saying they cost too much to maintain, but poor stakeholder relationships can end up costing more than ever imagined when they are ignored.

Stakeholders

Stakeholders are defined as anyone who can or does have influence over, or is influenced by, the company, organization, or brand. Any individual or group who has a "stake" in the company can influence its success or failure.

Stakeholder relationships are more costly to ignore than to address.

Of course, some stakeholders have more influence than others; but each group contributes to or takes away from the bottom line in some capacity. Though they may be numerous, each group plays a different role in the success of the whole. Decision makers who choose to ignore these often-complex relationships are headed for rough waters.

Today's demanding consumers

Today's consumers are much more demanding than they were only five years ago. They want increasingly more personalized offerings. And they are willing to pay a premium price for them. In fact, many will not settle for less.

Companies that are enjoying success today are the ones that are not only paying attention to the changing times, but also paying the financial costs of developing and maintaining strong relationships with bolder and more informed consumers.

Building relationships

Companies that are enjoying success today are the ones that are not only paying attention to the changing times, but also paying the financial costs of developing and maintaining strong relationships with bolder and more informed consumers.

Of course, this idea of building relationships is not a new or revolutionary concept, nor simply a clever term that companies tack onto their specialty credential lists. Some say the idea has been around since the beginning of commerce.

Early relationship-building consisted of Mom seeing something she wanted. She already knew the clerks; they knew her. She trusted the store and the products. Everything was produced, marketed, and sold locally. Mass media allowed local products to go national and national products to go global, but moms are still shopping and still want to trust the products and companies they support.

The driving assumption is that if good relationships are built, profitable transactions will follow. The goal of relationship building is to provide long-term benefits to stakeholders.

Successful companies are increasingly moving away from a focus on individual transactions and more toward a focus on building value-laden relationships with stakeholders. And they are paying whatever price it takes to get them there.

Are stakeholders worth the investments?

But who are these stakeholders who are worth such an investment? And how can a company even begin to address the needs of so many different interests and groups? Part of the answer is actually buried in the question. The first step in making relationships worth the financial risk many corporate leaders think they are is to identify the importance of each stakeholder group.

Recognizing the importance of stakeholders

The first and most important step in building strong stakeholder relationships is to recognize the various stakeholders who can affect the bottom line, either directly or indirectly. In general, there is a tendency among companies to place great emphasis on communicating and growing relationships with those groups who have direct influence over the bottom line, but neglecting other stakeholders such as employees, media, or even strategic partners.

Ever thought ill of a whole chain of stores just because one clerk was rude to you?

By ignoring other groups or failing to cultivate relationships with them, an organization can end up alienating them, making them feel unappreciated and antagonistic toward the company. Ever thought ill of a whole chain of stores just because one clerk was rude to you? Ever wish your strategic partners would present the same image of your company that you have worked so hard to convey? Who can say they have never been influenced by negative (or positive) press coverage? Stakeholders are powerful allies for a company or brand. But they can be dangerous foes, as well.

Listing your stakeholders

To recognize your various stakeholders, try listing all the stakeholders you can imagine who do or could have any influence over or be influenced by your company or brand. Conduct a thorough stakeholder audit by doing the below exercises:

To meet a need means to know the need. Knowing the need means knowing the stakeholders.

- Make a laundry list of everyone who has a stake in the organization.
- Describe the benefits that the stakeholder receives.
- Detail the benefits your company receives from each stakeholder group, both directly and indirectly.
- Analyze the state of the relationship today and note where you would like it to be.
- Go back and prioritize them based on the power of influence each has.

Recognizing stakeholder roles

Recognizing the importance of the various roles played by these stakeholder groups will lead to a more profitable organization. Knowing the concerns, needs, and desires of the people who affect the business will help you anticipate those needs and form an action plan for fixing or addressing their concerns.

It is not enough to know who your stakeholders are and why they are important. To build relationships that will add to the equity of a company, the smart leader must go beyond knowing the importance of stakeholders and commit the time and resources necessary to understand what those stakeholders need to make them loyal and satisfied advocates.

Communicating with stakeholders

No relationship can succeed without communication. Whether it is a personal, family, or business relationship, in order for a strong bond to be formed and maintained, each party involved must feel they are getting what they want out of the relationship.

Revisit the stakeholder audit and write down what each group wants or needs out of the relationship. Customers want good products, services, and prices; employees want security, fair compensation, and good working conditions; stockholders want incredible dividends; the media want good stories; strategic partners want successful partnerships, and so on.

Customers want good products, services, and prices; employees want security, fair compensation, and good working conditions; stakeholders want incredible dividends; the media wants good stories; strategic partners want successful partnerships, and so on. Nobody said it would be easy!

Your wants and needs

Just as each group has wants and needs from your company, you will have different wants and needs from them.

211

You obviously want the company to succeed. Each of these groups will have to play a part in accomplishing that success.

It is helpful to be aware of what each wants from you and what you want from them. You can then make informed decisions for smart budget allocation, management decisions, and marketing communications campaigns.

Streamline efforts to communicate

When you know what each group wants, you can streamline efforts to communicate that fulfilled desire to them. Be sure to stay consistent in communication, but tailor each situation to the desires and needs of that stakeholder group. They will feel more satisfied and therefore contribute their part to the success of your company.

Take advantage of every opportunity to reinforce the relationship by communicating with them regularly with the same familiar look and feel.

Be careful; do not ask for feedback if you are not prepared to answer quickly.

Feedback

It is also important to give stakeholders a way to communicate back to you. Feedback is often overlooked and even ignored by decision makers. But just try to have a personal relationship with any human where you do all the talking and none of the listening. It just does not work.

The same is true for stakeholder relationships. Provide regular feedback mechanisms that foster two-way communication. Clearly posting contact information on every piece of communication that goes out is one way to encourage feedback. Others include regular research among various groups, open phone lines for call-in concerns, quick response to questions and complaints, and even old-fashioned suggestion boxes. The Internet is a perfect place to solicit feedback from stakeholders.

But, be careful; do not ask for feedback if you are not prepared to answer quickly. Slow response can actually reverse any good the feedback opportunity might have created in the beginning.

Meeting the needs of stakeholders

A timely response will show commitment to the well-being of the various stakeholder groups. After they have been recognized and have had the chance to communicate with the organization, the relationship that has taken such time and effort to cultivate will fall by the wayside unless attention is paid to what has been learned from the process.

Finding ways to accommodate stakeholders' concerns and needs in the fundamental strategic planning of the organization will be the follow-through that allows for relationships to flourish. The goals and vision of the organization must be set in a way that leads to the most prosperous relationships. This may mean a departure from traditional methods of managing the business by shifting attention and funding to communication and programs designed specifically for growing relationships.

Making it work may mean a departure from traditional methods of managing the business by shifting attention and funding to communication and programs designed specifically for growing relationships.

213

Try forming measurable objectives for each of the top five stakeholder groups.

When the stakeholders see their needs and wants are being met, they will be more likely to contribute additional effort or money to their role as stakeholder. When that happens, the bottom line becomes clear: strong relationships are good for the bottom line. With each group contributing more, financial success will follow.

Stakeholders are lifeblood of organization

It has been said that stakeholders are the lifeblood of any organization. If that is true, it is absolutely critical to be in good standing with them. Cultivating relationships with so many stakeholder groups will take many resources and will certainly not happen overnight. But this is one area of investment companies in the 21st century cannot afford to ignore.

It has been said that stakeholders are the lifeblood of any organization. If that is true, it is absolutely critical to be in good standing with them.

With savvy consumers, increased competition, and growing noise in the marketplace, loyalty through relationships will be the differentiating factor that separates a strong bottom line from the bottom of the heap.

(Janella Griggs is Relationship Marketing Director for The Creative Alliance, a creative marketing and business development firm near Denver. She has a Master's Degree in Integrated Marketing Communications and specializes in strategic planning and stakeholder relationship building.)

214

26

Keeping Score for Your Business

**Good scorekeeping is important and beneficial,
but only if you have a purpose.**

By Elmer O. Bley

A very successful salesman once told me that when he first started to sell he would get in front of a prospective customer, tell him all his products and services, watch for a gleam in the man's eyes, and then focus on that product to hopefully score a sale. The only problem was many times he didn't get that gleam in the man's eye, didn't score, and didn't make a sale.

In too many cases the financial data provided to business owners and managers is begging to have the question asked, "What do you need?" or "Who is serving whom?"

He later learned that he needed to ask a series of questions related to the prospect's need. Once he identified the needs, he sought to provide products or services that responded to those needs. Often though, owners or managers buy services through employees or outside professionals and do not get what they need. Owners and managers need to get adequate financial information so that they can manage well.

In too many cases the financial data provided to business owners and managers is begging to have the question asked, "What do you need?" or "Who is serving whom?"

Accounting methods

Recently, I looked at a rather modern accounting textbook that raised the dilemma between preparing financial statements based on the way deals were analyzed versus the method used for record keeping and subsequent performance that was more tax oriented.

Is the financial data that you receive as practical, useful, and comprehensible as it needs to be?

Similarly, I had a conversation with a college accounting professor who revealed that it really did not make any difference in his view as to how overhead was distributed among departments. The allocation method might be used, or the specific usage method might be used; it had to get distributed in some manner.

Well, maybe it does make a difference in both cases.

Textbook situation

In the textbook situation, a manager will be held to a different basis of accountability than that on which the transaction was acquired. A typical illustration is the company that acquired several new units during a fiscal year. The financial information was prepared on the basis that the depreciation for book purposes would be the same as for tax purposes. The result from acquiring all of the new units over a short period of time was a very high depreciation charge for this department's operation. Therefore, the net income was severely reduced despite very good performance, and all according to plan.

The manager of the area was frustrated by the reported results of the operations because his managers would not be entitled to bonuses as a result of the accelerated depreciation used for tax purposes. Therefore, he had to do his own number keeping to convince his boss that his managers were doing a good job, and thus should be compensated for the job they were doing. Bonuses ended up being calculated without the results of the depreciation.

Now who is keeping score for whom?

Professor situation

In the situation with the professor, it is one thing to assign costs on the basis of usage, but quite another thing to totally distribute overhead costs based on other ratios. Using this latter method, the manager who is being held accountable to a level of profitability, which might be the basis for a bonus, might have his operating results going up or down because someone in charge of overhead had a big party.

Do you think the manager will have fun explaining that to his wife?

Resolving the issue

The unresolved issue in the textbook mentioned above is whether the information prepared for the owners and managers is going to satisfy their needs or the technical tax issues.

This issue is not a new one. A similar situation occurred when the investment credit was first born. There were great discussions in high places as to whether investment credits should be amortized over the life of the asset that gave rise to that credit, or whether that credit should immediately fall to the bottom as a reduction of taxes and an increase in income.

Act of Congress

It took an Act of Congress to dictate how this would be handled in the marketplace so that the immediate impact of the investment credit would improve earnings, increased per share value, and therefore help the economy as the tax credit was originally intended.

Therefore, if a company had paid a bonus at the time the credit was generated, and subsequently sold the asset, it might find that it had overpaid the bonus. Like that result?

What one could learn out of all this is that legislative accounting was not necessarily the best answer for good economic and managerial accounting—economic impact was realized only if the asset was kept long enough to survive the recovery period. Otherwise, a pro rata portion of the credit would be reversed, reducing earnings that had already been booked.

Therefore, if a company had paid a bonus at the time the credit was generated, and subsequently sold the asset, it might find that it had overpaid the bonus. Like that result?

Statistical information

Many years ago, when the SEC was revising the bank holding companies regulations, statistical information was being requested by a large variety of categories. When the bankers complained that the information was not available, the regulators were surprised to find that few banks managed on the basis of bank-wide statistics. They were managed by areas of responsibility, and certain yields were only a byproduct of what various systems would generate.

No one person in a large banking institution, particularly one that is operating under a decentralized management style, is responsible for the entire yield on all the loans or for any particular kind of loan. You must have information to manage by areas of responsibility in formats that parallel the way managers make deals.

Smaller companies not different

Unfortunately, smaller companies are not really different. The same battle as to who needs the information and for what purpose continues to loom in the marketplace today. Financial data is prepared to pay taxes or for the banks, but does the man who is paying the bill get the information he needs? In many cases it seems that he has been forgotten, not to mention the fact that he does not know he has any options.

There has to be a better way

I have been coaching companies to manage better for the past twelve years, and invariably financial measurement problems appear. There has to be a better way, and some businesses are finding it.

You must have information to manage by areas of responsibility in formats that parallel the way managers make deals.

Not the way

One example is that of contractor X. In his company, all union dues that were based on labor were included in general and administrative (G&A) expenses. Workman's compensation insurance was also included in G&A expenses because it was insurance; and all of the FICA taxes were included in G&A because they were payroll taxes.

Still the owner could not understand why his G&A expenses went up just because he hired more people to work in the field. To him, that should not have affected his G&A expenses. When he bid a job, he included all the payroll expenses in the cost of the job.

Many contractors shrug their shoulders at the confusing bottom line numbers, then file the report in the bottom drawer.

The problem is compounded in a labor intensive business if the workmen's compensation deposit is just amortized over a period of months with no calculation related to the volume of payroll. The owner then wakes up to a possible large premium adjustment upon audit that significantly changes his economic result for the last year.

So how is such an owner ever to compare his bidding ratios to his monthly financial information? Does he just read the bottom line, shrug his shoulders at the mystic, and file the reports in the bottom drawer? Many do, but you do not have to. There is a better way that will allow you to manage closer to your potential.

A better way

In another situation an owner wanted to reward his managers based on performance. A considerable period of time elapsed to get the systems in place so that the measurement of the managers' areas of responsibility was reliable. Nobody really got serious about the numbers until bonuses started to accrue based on the numbers. When they did, the results in the target department increased immensely. The results were amazing.

Everybody becomes conscious of what is being charged to their department when bonuses are in the air.

To be sure, some of the good results might be coming from getting the accounting straightened out, but all of a sudden financial information for each department became extremely important. Better deals were being made. Closer attention was being paid to warranty credits, etc. Everyone became conscious of what was being charged to his or her department.

The managers of the departments are now doing a much better job of managing their departments, since how much goes into their pocket at the end of year is dependent on how well that department does. This company is now getting the financial information that it needs and the managers and owner are getting information they understand and can use.

When good information is not produced

When the financial information does not produce good economic information useful to their audience, good managers may, and usually will, find another way of getting the furnished information set aside so as to get the benefits to which they are economically entitled.

Good managers will get the pay benefits necessary to keep their team together, or they will move on. Good managers will not be held up too long by unrealistic financial data.

Information now easy to get

There was a time in life when crunching out another set of depreciation numbers or the likes was really time consuming and expensive and one questioned whether or not it was necessary. Today with computers, that is certainly not the case.

Good managers will get the pay benefits necessary to keep their team together, or they will move on.

The real question now is one of purpose and philosophy. Managers and owners of businesses, with appropriate professional assistance, need to set that purpose and philosophy.

So, if you are an owner or manager, are you getting the information you need to manage well and to your potential? Are you asking the right questions?

Seven questions to consider asking

1. Do your financial statements give you information so that you know you are pricing correctly?

2. If you sell or deal in more than one product, do you know the gross profit ratios on the various products?

3. Does your gross profit information in your financial statements include the same data you include when bidding a job?

4. If you are not making the profits your pricing is supposed to give you, do you know why? What needs to change?

5. Are the results you are getting economically useful, or do they just satisfy smart tax accounting?

6. Could you pay your managers and yourself bonuses based on the information you get?

7. If you manage two or more legal entities in related
    businesses that interact with each other, do you ever
    see the combined result as though there were one?

The age-old question of accounting methods raised by
the accounting textbook still exists, and the question still has
to be answered.

Business owners and managers

Business owners and managers, make sure you are
getting the financial information you need. That is, after all,
the main purpose for keeping score.

Taxes and financial reporting are necessary, but they are
not the highest priority. Make sure you get the information
you need to guide you to manage well—so that you manage
closer to your potential.

*(Elmer O. Bley had a short career in public accounting and five years
on the staff of the Securities and Exchange Commission before spending over
twenty years as the Chief Financial Officer of a major bank holding
company in Maryland. For the last twelve years he has been the principal in
Master Designers, Inc.)*

27

Profit Sharing— Does It Pay?

Finding out what really works and does not work in profit sharing.

By Michael Zigarelli, Ph.D.

Beyond the justice dimension of profit sharing, let's think about profit sharing's financial impact on an organization. Sharing profits should both increase employee productivity and decrease turnover, according to widely advanced theories.[1]

Linking part of one's pay to firm performance could elicit more effort from that individual, say the theorists. And, because workers are rewarded as a group under this program, they may be more willing to share information and to operate as a team.

According to theory, sharing profits should both increase employee productivity and decrease turnover.

Regarding turnover, since profit sharing tends to elevate employee compensation to a level that is above the market (an "efficiency wage" in economist-speak), employees may be more reluctant to leave the firm. Moreover, above-market wages may also reduce shirking of duties, since the cost to the employee of being fired is not just a job search, but probably a lower wage at the end of that search.

Qualified findings

Well, these are theories. But we have a particular reason to be skeptical here. We know from experience that such hypotheses often originate in political and social agendas rather than economic ones. Ivory-tower types and policy wonks regularly advocate profit sharing under the guise of enhancing organizational performance, but it may be little more than a transparent initiative for social re-engineering. So when one sifts through the voluminous research and commentary on profit sharing, one should be cautious to separate the wheat from the chaff.

Of course, there is some wheat, or substance, in the research. Even though the empirical work has not yet conclusively demonstrated a clear, causal effect on productivity, turnover, and profits,[2] a few large-sample, well-designed studies exist that point us toward preliminary conclusions about what works and does not with profit sharing programs.[3] Moreover, their findings are bolstered by an abundance of anecdotal evidence.

The research confirms that where employees do not perceive a direct linkage between their effort and the size of their profit-sharing check, their effort and decisions to stay with the organization will be unaffected by any profit-sharing plan.

226

The downside

On the downside, these studies show that profit sharing can degenerate into nothing more than an added cost of operations. The research confirms that where employees do not perceive a direct linkage between their effort and the size of their profit-sharing check, their effort and decisions to stay with the organization will be unaffected by any profit-sharing plan. Moreover, even if there is a perceived linkage, a small profit-sharing bonus has little impact on individual outcomes. Similarly, deferred bonus (e.g., profits put into the employee's pension account rather than offered as cash), no matter the size, has no discernible effect on current productivity.

Profit sharing factors:

#1—company size

#2—cost monitoring

#3—turnover

That may seem like common sense. Behaviors are highly correlated with valuable and immediate rewards whether we're training a dog, raising a toddler, or managing employees. However, the simplicity of this principle appears to escape those designing many of the profit-sharing plans. According to a 1997 study, 42 percent of companies still base rewards on criteria that employees cannot directly influence (e.g., stock prices, earnings per share).[4]

Effective profit-sharing programs

Notwithstanding the pitfalls, though, profit-sharing programs can work and have worked. Here are a few factors that the empirical studies have identified as influencing their success.

227

Does profit sharing increase profits?—the jury in the research community still remains out, but anecdotal evidence suggests significant effects on corporate financial performance.

First, company size appears to be an important variable in the equation. Smaller companies (775 employees or fewer) tend to experience productivity increases of between 11 and 17 percent, whereas in larger firms, the effects range from 0-7 percent. Seemingly, a larger workforce makes the individual behavior-bonus linkage more tenuous and can create more of a "free rider" problem.

Second, profit sharing tends to be especially useful where costs of monitoring employees are high. As is true of any effective pay-for-performance system, when employees perceive that real and meaningful rewards will flow from augmented effort, they will require less supervision of their diligence. The research has correlated profit-sharing with dramatic reductions of supervisory costs.

Third, the best empirical work has demonstrated that profit sharing can lead to lower turnover, especially where profit sharing substitutes for part of base pay, rather than being gravy on top of base pay. The precise cause of this is still a matter of debate, but from a statistical perspective, the relationship is undeniable.

And as to the ultimate question in the boardroom—does profit sharing increase profits?—the jury in the research community still remains out. But a plethora of anecdotal evidence suggests significant effects on corporate financial performance. Here is but one testimony to profit sharing's impressive potential to both resuscitate and reinforce a business.

A case study: Cin-Made

Robert Frey had purchased Cin-Made, a small manufacturing company that was replete with labor problems: astronomical labor costs, contentious union-management relations, an embarrassing 75 percent on-time shipping rate, and a dismal and volatile bottom line. Frey had several options, according to prevailing management theory. Here's what he did.

To remedy some of Cin-Made's financial woes, Frey purchased faster machinery and sought wage concessions of 25 percent. His three dozen workers, whose jobs had not changed in decades, outright rejected the new technology, ostensibly because they feared injury with faster equipment. And as far as wage concessions, the knee-jerk response was a prolonged strike. Eventually, they came back to work at a 12.5 percent pay cut, but he admitted his victory here only won him, "a factory full of angry, defeated, employees determined to oppose any innovation, and grieve every tiny infraction of the letter of the contract."[5]

> The owner tried something radical. He proposed giving employees 30 percent of pretax profits and keeping the books open for the union scrutiny.

Through these cost-reduction initiatives, Cin-Made's profits stabilized a bit. But Frey knew that he had yet to identify a long-run solution for the company. So he tried something radical. He proposed giving employees 30 percent of pretax profits and keeping the books open for the union scrutiny. He held monthly state-of-the-business meetings with employees to let them know how the company was doing. And he gave them more managerial responsibilities (e.g., problem solving, cost cutting, allocating overtime, interviewing applicants) to give them a personal feel for management's concerns.

In essence, his strategy was to sensitize workers to the financial and marketing realities of the business, and to give them a stake in the outcomes. He sought to achieve that elusive objective of aligning worker and employer interests.

Lackluster beginning

The first four years of this new approach met with lackluster results. Thirty percent of small profits translated into small bonuses and little change in the work culture. Since 1989, though, Cin-Made's profit has been strong and, consequently, annual profit-sharing checks have represented on average a 36-percent increase in pay.

In a factory of a few dozen employees, the linkage between individual effort and bonus size was readily apparent, and as Frey's employees began realizing the fruits of their labors, their commitment and contribution increased commensurately.

Their mind-set has been transformed. They think like managers, they consider themselves to be on the same side of the table as their CEO, and they work collectively to enlarge the pie for everyone involved.

Results today

Today, Cin-Made boasts a 98 percent on-time delivery record, a productivity level up 30 percent from the mid-1980's, very low absenteeism, and a workforce that meticulously monitors waste and temporary employees. Strict adherence to job descriptions is a thing of the past, grievances are down to one to two per year, and labor relations are peaceable. Tri-annual wage negotiations proceed from the premise that any increase in fixed wages or benefits comes out of profit sharing, so the negotiations tend to be amiable. According to Frey, this chunk of money belongs entirely to the employees, so they can have it in whatever form they want it.[6]

These employees chose to perpetuate and depend on the pay-for-performance system. Their mind-set has been transformed. They think like managers, they consider themselves to be on the same side of the table as their CEO, and they work collectively to enlarge the pie for everyone involved.

A win-win solution

It would intolerably strain the scriptural text to say that there is any mandate in Proverbs for profit sharing. However, profit sharing does seem to be a legitimate extension of the prudent teaching that we honor God by sharing our resources with those who have little. That would seem particularly the case for the lowest-level employees.

Moreover, but in our context secondarily, it can also be an effective business tool, since, implemented properly, sharing profits can align the interest of employees with those of the employer and the company's owners. It therefore represents a scripturally sound win-win solution. Profit sharing is a reward strategy that both satisfies employee economic needs and encourages them to care more about customer service, cost containment, and quality.

Taken from: *Management by Proverbs*, by Michael A. Zigarelli, Ph.D. Copyright, 1999, Michael A. Zigarelli. Moody Press. Used by permission.

(Michael A. Zigarelli, Ph.D., an Associate Professor of Management at Regent University in Virginia Beach, has extensively studied management, law, and ethics. He is the author of three books: including Management By Proverbs and Can They Do That? A Guide to Your Rights on the Job. Dr Zigarelli lives in Virginia with his wife Tara and their three children.)

Notes

1. For some of the better theoretical work on this subject, see Martin L. Weitzman and Douglas L. Kruse, "Profit Sharing and Productivity," in Alan S. Binder, ed., *Paying for Productivity* (Washington D.C.: The Brookings Institution 1990); and Douglas L. Kruse, "Profit Sharing and Productivity: Microeconomic Evidence from the United States," *The Economic Journal*, 102, no. 1 (January 1992): 24-36.

2. The most comprehensive empirical treatment of this topic to date is Douglas L. Kruse, *Profit Sharing: Does It Make a Difference?* (Kalamazoo, Mich.: W.E. Upjohn Institute, 1993).

3. In addition to Kruse's 1992 and 1993 studies (see notes 1 and 2), other work used for this section includes Sushil Wadhwani and Martin Wall, "The Effects of Profit Sharing on Employment, Wages, Stock Returns and Productivity: Evidence from UK Microdata," *The Economic Journal*, 100, no. 3 (March 1990): 1-17; and Felix R. RitzRoy and K. Kraft, "Cooperation, Productivity, and Profit Sharing,"*Quarterly Journal of Economics*, 102, no. 1, (1987): 23-25.

4. Julie Johnsson, "Bonus Bust: Firms Fumble Cash Payout," *Crain's Chicago Business*, 1 December 1997.

5. Robert Frey, "The Empowered and the Glory: A Firm's Turbulent Turnaround," *The Washington Post*, 26 December 1993, H1.

6. Frey, "The Empowered and the Glory," *The Washington Post*, 26 December 1993, H1; and "CEO Finds Empowerment Pays," *The Cincinnati Enquirer*, 29 July 1993, B9.

28

How to avoid a financial disaster

Preparing for success must include being ready for disasters.

by Steve Marr

You answer the phone and are notified that you've lost your largest customer. You open the morning newspaper and learn that a major investor has filed bankruptcy. Or maybe you turn on your car radio and are stunned by reports of economic bad news that will drastically cut your company's sales.

No one ever expects disaster to strike, but such devastating events hit almost every business at one time or another. And your leadership in time of crisis will spell the difference between victory and defeat for your company.

These nightmare scenarios may seem remote possibilities for your business. No one ever expects disaster to strike, but such devastating events hit almost every business at one time or another. And your leadership in time of crisis will spell the difference between victory and defeat for your company.

At a point of crisis, every leader must evaluate three important questions about his business:

1. What is our company's mission statement and key objective?

2. How long can we survive in the current situation?

3. What is our best plan for saving the company?

Three keys to getting started

Asking these crucial questions will set in motion your course for survival, and will prepare you to take the actions necessary to save your business.

1. Company mission statement

A company mission statement is the starting point for surviving any crisis. If you don't have a mission statement, now is the time to cast a vision for your organization. Focus on stating the reason you are in business, the product or service you provide, and the customers you serve. This may prove difficult under pressure, but you cannot navigate troubled water without a clear map that allows you to plot a route to travel.

Resist the temptation to be optimistic. Only an accurate, realistic assessment will be helpful during a crisis.

Scripture states that "without a vision, the people will perish." Likewise, without a vision of your company's mission, you and your staff will be without direction. Any effort spent without a clear vision is wasted.

2. Evaluation of business survival potential

Equally important to your business is an honest evaluation of how long your business can survive in its current state. It is essential that you develop a realistic chart of income, expenses, and cash flow, and compare it to available business assets.

Resist the temptation to be optimistic. Only an accurate, realistic assessment will be helpful during a crisis.

3. Realistic financial diagnosis

Finally, with your mission statement and a realistic financial diagnosis, you are ready to develop a survival curve, plotting the cash flow before your business runs out of cash.

Two options typically present themselves: increase revenue or reduce operating expenses. A key factor to remember is that increasing revenue quickly in crisis to make up for a major shortfall rarely works. Don't fall victim to the wish of finding revenue under a rug. You're better off reducing expenses, which provides the quickest opportunity to improve your survival curve.

Two options in tight times:

1—increase revenue

2—reduce operating expenses

Once circumstances assessed

Once you've assessed your circumstances, it's time to examine your business with an eye toward survival. An apt analogy is to think of your business as a tree, with many branches suffering from severe drought. If you do nothing, the tree will likely die because it is unable to support all its branches and leaves during the drought.

In business as in nature, some branches must die to allow the tree to live. Rather than do nothing, a better course of action is to evaluate the water shortfall and preempt the death of the tree by pruning branches, even healthy growth, in order to save the tree. In extreme cases, all the branches must be cut to save the tree.

Three keys for avoiding financial disaster

1. Company mission statement
2. Evaluation of business survival potential
3. Realistic financial diagnosis

Work must match mission statement

Your job now is to examine each element of your business to determine the elements that fit your mission statement. Use a critical eye to create a list of the work exactly matching your mission statement, make another list of functions that partly fit your mission, and make yet a third listing those that are off target in light of your stated business objective. Keep the lists available as you begin formulating your plan for survival.

Focus on the storm

With your initial assessment completed, it is time to begin planning your company's recovery strategy. Three key elements must be kept in constant focus as you plan and work to save your business:

#1—cash flow

#2—expenses

#3—product quality

It is important to focus your energy on these factors first. In time of crisis, focus is critical. If you become distracted, return to these foundational issues and be sure that they are working to accomplish and support your mission statement. You should begin your planning by examining how each of your company's products and services fits with your mission statement. By immediately eliminating those that do not support your mission statement, you can achieve quick progress in your three priority areas.

These three elements will figure prominently in your decision-making. You should determine what progress can be made in each area, listing all relevant actions that can be taking to achieve each priority.

Cash flow

If cash flow is critical, you can work with accounts to insure prompt payment and initiate immediate past-due procedures. You could also attempt to obtain advances from accounts or create discounts for immediate payment. If feasible, offer to pick up checks or deliver billing invoices, and attempt to speed shipments and delivery to customers to facilitate incoming cash. The key is to prepare a multi-phased plan with complete focus on the critical issues.

Expenses

The second critical issue is expenses, which represents the most necessary adjustment in a crisis. When it comes to expenses, you are in control. Begin by evaluating every expense, both large and small, to determine the immediate impact each has on serving the customers and manufacturing your product. You can first eliminate non-essential expenses, such as travel and capital spending, then move to cutting variable expenses incurred based on business volume.

By immediately eliminating the products and services that do not support your mission statement, you can achieve quick progress in your three priority areas.

Product quality

Finally, product quality must be maintained and any loss will compound your difficulties. In today's business environment, customers quickly notice deterioration of product or service quality. Reliability always sells in the marketplace, and consistency will assist in retaining customers. Any cost savings generated by cutting corners will be quickly offset by lost business— business you can not easily replace.

The hard part is cutting staff and wages, but before you do, make sure you have an accurate and objective view of your financial deficit.

Hard choices

Up to this point, most of the decisions you've made have been relatively easy: cutting non-essential spending and weeding out activities that don't fit your mission statement. Now, the decisions start getting tougher, to the point of potentially cutting staff or wages. It is important to calculate the remaining shortfall in your survival curve to get an accurate picture of what remains to be done to survive.

Staff reduction

Before you make these hard choices, review the staffing required to provide service or product with the lower volume of work. Staff reductions are normally required to reduce cost under crisis circumstances. It's important to consider moving beyond lower-level staff reductions to considering lowering management personnel costs as well.

For example, you may have a department with 20 employees, including one manager and two supervisors. Work in that department is down 50 percent. You could lay off 10 lower-level staff, keeping the three management positions.

Yet, it might be more cost-effective to lay off eight staff and the two supervisors, if the remaining manager can adequately oversee the department's operation. In this situation, reducing low-cost staff will not generate maximum wage savings.

Wage reduction

Wage reductions can be another effective cost-cutting measure. You may consider wage reductions as high as 15 percent until the crisis passes. A sign of leadership would be to first reduce your own salary and that of your senior managers. If given an option and an honest explanation, most workers will agree to short-term reductions to help the business survive. It is unwise, however, to offer salary reductions to avoid the problem of trimming excess staff.

Eight points for dealing with staff during crisis

1. Welcome their input and help
2. Show how success will be achieved and measured
3. Be direct
4. Create sense of urgency, not panic
5. Make sure staff understands importance of unity
6. Remember importance of staff
7. Share the victories
8. Praise the Lord liberally

Your Survival Plan

It is now time to move beyond assessment to formulating a plan for survival. Although the situation requires leadership, you shouldn't try to save your business alone. Scripture reminds us of the need for both leadership and wise counsel. As it states in Proverbs 11:14, "Where there is no guidance, the people fall, but in abundance of counselors there is victory."

Once you've drafted a plan, allow one or more trusted, experienced, and godly individuals to review it. Ask for honest evaluation and give significant weight to the counsel. Others can be far more objective and can provide tremendous insight, especially when you are under pressure. You should be sure to ask each advisor to challenge your work and assumptions. Revisit and revise your plan until you feel comfortable that it is workable and effective.

Implement your plan quickly

Once you have a plan, implement it quickly. As the Scripture warns, "Do not stand in the fork of the road" (paraphrase of *Obadiah 1:14*). Two factors will work against you if you delay or implement your plan piecemeal. First, the quick benefit of cost savings will be lost, causing your plan to fail not because it was flawed but because of slow implementation. Second, staff hate to wait for the other shoe to drop. By now, morale is already stressed, but it will plummet if more staff reductions are seen looming on the horizon. It's best to work quickly, completely, and thoroughly.

Once you have a plan, implement it quickly!

Measure your progress

Along the way, be sure to have benchmarks to measure progress by both time and amount. In an emergency, time is not on your side. Progress measured by time will be equally important as progress measured by dollar amounts, and both require equal importance. The key is to have objective, measurable goals built into your survival plan. They will provide mile markers on your road to recovery.

Your staff is more likely to rally around a plan if they understand it and it makes sense to them.

Staff involvement

In a crisis situation, it is important to keep in mind that your business only runs because of the people involved. Staff members are more than numbers on a spreadsheet. They are individuals with concerns and feelings about the upheaval going on in the business. They are concerned about how it affects their lives, careers and families. At this time you need to meet with your staff to outline the situation as honestly as possible, as well as the progress that needs to be made. They need to know where the business is, how the situation developed, and how you plan to move forward and maintain the organization.

Here are eight points to keep in mind when dealing with staff during a crisis:

1. Welcome their input and help

Let them know you welcome their input and help. Bringing your staff in to discuss the solution develops a sense of ownership and loyalty. Often great ideas come from all levels of the company, not just from the boss. It's important to be willing to give and take, as long as you move toward your stated goals.

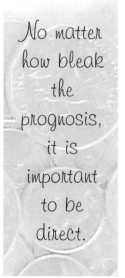

2. Show how success will be achieved and measured

As you explain the plan, be sure to show how success will be achieved and measured. Your staff is more likely to rally around a plan if they understand it and it makes sense to them. Explain to them how each can and must contribute to make the plan work. Your staff is likely to rally around a plan that makes sense and involves them.

3. Be direct

No matter how bleak the prognosis, it is important to be direct. Your colleagues desire and deserve to hear and understand the truth.

4. Create sense of urgency, not panic

You should create a sense of urgency, but not of panic. Effective leadership requires you to inspire action while still keeping your cool. If your staff senses panic or pessimism on your part, your survival plan could quickly unravel.

5. Make sure staff understands importance of unity

Make sure your staff understands the importance of unity during the crisis. Monitor staff members to see that the effort of each is supporting your plan. If anyone is not fully on board, or insists on arguing extensively, insist they join the team or leave the company. A leader must have full cooperation while digging out of a tough spot.

242

6. Remember importance of staff

Remember how important your staff is, in crisis and in the future of your business. You cannot do all the work yourself. Your key job is to write and monitor the plan, then keep everyone focused on the key tasks at hand.

7. Share the victories

Share the victories, both small and large, with the staff and celebrate together. This is not a time to be stingy with encouragement and praise. When the crisis passes, be sure to reward those who have assisted the recovery and paid some personal price in the process. Some ways to do this include bonuses, extra raises or other unexpected benefits.

8. Praise the Lord liberally

Give liberal praise to the Lord. Let your staff see your reliance on Him during difficulties, as He gives you strength and answers prayer. Times of trouble and crisis can bring great glory to the Lord.

Leadership was the key to building your business into a success. It has been essential to keeping it running well and profitably during the good times. And it is that same leadership that will enable you to weather any storm, no matter how catastrophic it may seem when it first hits.

(Steve Marr is President of Master Builders Management, which consults with organizations for strategic effectiveness. His radio program, Business Proverbs, is heard on 160 stations internationally. Prior to full-time ministry, Steve was President of the fourth largest international trade company in the United States.)

29

Downsizing Done Right

When you've exhausted every option but downsizing, remember this: Do it the right way.

by Brian D. Molitor

Downsizing is a term that invokes powerful emotions in people today. For stockholders, the term sparks excitement as visions of increased profitability dance in their heads. The reaction of middle level managers is often one of disbelief as they mentally wrestle with the controlled chaos that a large reduction in manpower will bring into their work lives. Those who face the brunt of the workforce reductions are often left reeling from the shock of impending job loss and the resulting impact on their personal lives.

> Downsizing is the current word for an old fashioned layoff of significant numbers of blue or white-collar employees.

Downsizing

For anyone who may have been off the planet for a while, let's define our terms. Downsizing is the current word for an old fashioned layoff of significant numbers of blue or white-collar employees. Downsizing is an attempt to better an organization's competitiveness, and often comes in response to a change in profitability, loss of market share, new competition, increased operating costs, and so on.

Executives who must make the decision to downsize their organization are in a very difficult position. They were hired to increase the value of their company and, therefore, must make every attempt to maximize profitability. On the other hand, they are also entrusted with the lives and futures of the many people that work for them. This creates some classic conflicts between the executives' hearts and their heads.

Agonizing over downsizing

I have spoken with many executives who agonized over the decision to downsize. They struggle with the paradox that comes from having to hurt some employees to save the jobs of those who would remain. What will happen to the workers that so faithfully served the company for so long? How many children will not be able to attend college if dad or mom lose the job? Will some employees lose their homes without the paycheck from the company?

Executives agonize over the decision to lay off some employees to save the jobs of those who remain.

These executives also wrestle with the lack of assurance that downsizing is truly the best choice for the organization in the long run. What happens if their business takes an unexpected upturn in the near future? Will opportunities to expand and seize new markets be lost if the downsizing takes place? How will they ever replace the skills and knowledge that walk out the door when the workers leave? While it may not show on a ledger, each employee represents a huge financial investment that will be lost as a result of the downsizing. Does that make sense?

Over the years, I have observed downsizing efforts in government, industry, healthcare, and even in a variety of ministries. At times, I have had the opportunity to assist organizations in planning for their future when downsizing was unavoidable. Based upon these experiences, I have learned that there is a wrong way to downsize and, when no other option to increase competitiveness exists, there is a right way.

Downsizing done wrong

Here are five ways to handle downsizing guaranteed to ruin your reputation as a company and insure that your remaining employees will never trust you again.

Downsizing done wrong can ruin your reputation forever!

1. At first sign of downturn, lay off many employees

At the first sign of a business downturn, lay off many of your employees. By all means, don't take any risks with your bottom line. After all, if the down turn was temporary you can simply hire other workers, supervisors, managers, and executives who will step in and get the job done, right?

Five ways to do downsizing wrong

1. At first sign of a downturn, lay off many employees
2. Keep employees in dark
3. Trivialize the negative effects
4. Tell them how it will profit the company
5. Tell remaining employees they are lucky to have jobs

2. Keep employees in dark

After your decision to downsize has been made, but before the layoffs occur, be sure to keep your employees in the dark. Don't tell them the truth about the uncertainties of the future. Let rumors spread to create fear among your staff. If anything is shared about the impending downsizing, use half-truths and outright lies to keep people from being able to plan for their lives. After all, if they know that a layoff is going to occur, they might begin to steal company pens.

This approach should ensure that your workforce would spend hours each day worrying about what will happen, when it will happen, and who will be impacted. That is certainly better than having them focus on serving your customers.

3. Trivialize the negative effects

When you finally get around to telling people

Ten top upsizing challenges

1. Unique cultures (each company was different at its core)
2. Different approaches to relationships
3. Duplication of services & equipment
4. Differences in pay, benefit packages, how seniority is calculated, job classifications, and how hiring, firing and discipline are handled.
5. Duplicate CEOs (one must accept the lesser position of COO), managers, department supervisors, security officers and cafeteria managers
6. Resigning employees (who don't like the new management) and/or resentment (for being bypassed in the interview process)
7. Policies and manuals (must be rewritten)
8. Signs through the hallways and on city streets (must be updated to indicate that a new organization is now in existence)
9. Union contacts (need to be renegotiated by the new company leadership)
10. Moving offices and relocating people (can also confuse customers)

248

Five ways to do downsizing right

1. Make sure downsizing is necessary
2. Explore your options
3. Minimize negative impact
4. Communicate early and often
5. Treat remaining employees as valuable resources

about the downsizing, trivialize the negative effects of this decision on them. Remind them of other eras when workers really had it tough. One great strategy is to sternly tell them to quit whining, grow up, and move on with their lives. Do your best to ignore the fact that they have just spent many years helping your company to succeed.

Another strategy is the cheerfully instruct them to look on the bright side of things. Be sure and tell them that other people have it a lot worse than they do, and that the world is full of great opportunities.

4. Tell them how it will profit the company

In order to really destroy employee commitment, be sure to remind them of how this downsizing will make the company much more profitable, and how happy the stockholders will be as a result of the reduced costs. Just be sure to locate the back door to the room before you tell them—you will need it shortly.

5. Tell remaining employees they are lucky to have jobs

Finally, after the downsizing has been carried out, tell the remaining employees how lucky they are to still have jobs.

Subtly threaten them if they get out of line or ask for anything new. Show no compassion for those who have been displaced. This will really help your remaining workers know your true character.

Downsizing done right

Here are five ways to handle downsizing that will help to protect your reputation as a company and insure that your remaining employees will continue to trust and respect you.

1. Make sure downsizing necessary

Make sure that the downsizing is truly necessary and no other options exist. Do not react to temporary downturns in your profitability, sales, etc. Be sure that you are responding to a long-term trend before you take the drastic step of dismissing your most valuable resources.

Remember that the way you treat the employees who are going to be laid off will speak volumes to those who will remain.

2. Explore your options

Next, explore your options. Is it possible to have a temporary layoff, rather than a permanent one? Could some employees take a leave of absence rather than be dismissed? Can you transfer some employees to new positions? Is it possible to offer early retirement for senior employees and/or separation packages for interested employees?

3. Minimize negative impact

Next, do all you can to minimize the negative impact on your employees who will be displaced. Assist by providing services to help them find other employment. Secure counselors who can help employees work through the pain and fear of change. Provide good employees with professional letters of recommendation and referrals to other companies.

Realize that a 20% reduction in your workforce means a 20% increase in workload for those who remain.

Whenever possible, offer severance packages and/or extend healthcare benefits so the employee's families are cared for. Create support groups for employees where they can vent their frustrations, talk about their fears and gain strength from others.

Realize that the whole person's body, soul, and spirit are affected by such a traumatic change in life. Establish prayer meetings to provide people with earthly support for today and some heavenly guidance for their future.

4. Communicate early and often

Also, once the decision has been made to downsize, communicate early and often with all affected people. Tell employees everything about the layoff that you possibly can and allow them to ask questions. Honesty and empathy are keys to all communications. Acknowledge feelings of hurt, anger, fear, and frustration.

Remember that the way you treat the employees who are going to be laid off will speak volumes to those who will remain. If you are deceptive, underhanded or cruel, you probably won't have to worry about another round of downsizing—the employees who survived the first round of layoffs will begin to look for other employment immediately.

5. Treat remaining employees as valuable resources

Finally, after the downsizing has occurred, treat your remaining employees as if they are the most valuable resources that you have, because that is precisely what they are. Realize that a 20% reduction in your workforce means a 20% increase in workload for those who remain.

It is very likely that your employees' work loads were full to begin with, so be sensitive to potential problems with stress, burnout, and other negative impacts on employee's families as overtime increases.

Do it right

Downsizing is an unfortunate aspect of organizational life. When handled properly, you can: maintain a reputation for being both professional and fair, secure employee commitment, and position yourself for growth when business picks up again in the future. If you have to downsize—do it right.

(Brian D. Molitor is founder and CEO of Molitor International., an international consulting and training firm. He has authored numerous books and training manuals on managing change, leadership, team building, problem solving and executive level leadership coaching. He lives in Michigan with his wife and four children.)

Business
Reference Section

Authors, Businesses & Ministries Represented

Andrews, A. L.
Building on the Rock Ministries, with A.L. Andrews as founder and CEO, provides seminars on starting and operating a business and effective business planning. Building on the Rock provides practical Biblical principles for Building Thriving Businesses—God's Way. For more information, write to: 44522 Lostwood Ave, Lancaster, CA 93534, fax: (661) 948-4133 or email: CEO@tceonline.com.

Baldwin, Robb W.
Portfolio Management & Research, a Florida based Registered Investment Advisory firm, provides investment management and advisory services for individual and institutional accounts. Affiliated with Fidelity Investments and Trade-PMR Discount Brokerage, PM&R, Inc., uses a no-fee fund network consisting of over 3,000 investment companies and can be reached at: (352) 332-1938, 6777 West Newberry Road, Gainesville, FL 32605 Attn. Robb, or www.tradepmr.com.

Ball, F. Nolan
The Rock of Panama City, Florida, under the leadership of Apostle F. Nolan Ball, is a church committed to establishing the five-fold ministry (apostles, prophets, evangelists, pastors and teachers). The church is located at 2413 North Harris Avenue, Panama City, FL 32405. Phone: (850) 785-7625. Email: therockpc@worldnet.att.net Website: therockofpanamacity.org.

Bley, Elmer O.
MASTER DESIGNERS, INC., founded by Elmer O. Bley, provides management coaching and chief financial officer services to business owners and managers. The firm seeks

to solve administrative problems, guide owners and managers to make wise, well- focused, long range decisions, so as to let owners and managers concentrate on doing what they do best. To contact MDI, write 4505 Fitch Ave., Baltimore, MD 21236, or e-mail elmero@freewwweb.com.

Brantley, George A.

The Rock of Gainesville, Florida, under Senior Pastor George A. Brantley, has grown from five (his own family in 1987) to over 1200. The Rock is about being relevant to this generation. For more information, ph: (352)331-ROCK, fx: (352)331-9760, email: info@therockonline.com home page: www.therockonline.com or write: 9818 SW 24th Avenue, Gainesville, FL 32607.

Brown, Denny

JobSeekers, co-directed by Denny Brown, is an evangelistic ministry to men, led by volunteer businessmen, which encourages and assists unemployed and under employed businessmen in finding meaningful employment. JobSeekers was founded in Atlanta in 1991 and is dedicated to planting locally operated volunteer groups throughout the United States. For more information, see www.jobseekers.org or email: denny@jobseekers.org.

Dayton, Howard

Crown Ministries, founded in 1985, is an interdenomina-tional ministry that trains people in small group settings, under the direction of the local church, to apply the financial principles from the Bible to their everyday lives. For more information, call (407) 331-6000, write: 530 Crown Oak Centre Drive, Longwood, Florida 32750, or visit their web site at: www.crown.org.

Everett, R. Richard

The Everett Financial Group, Inc. has grown to be one of Connecticut's largest and most respected financial planning firms and offers securities through Securities Service Network, Inc., Member of the National Association of Securities Dealers (NASD) and the Securities Investors Protection Corporation (SIPC). For further information: 202 State Street in North Haven, Connecticut 06473 Ph (203) 281-4661 or (800) 959-3582.

Fehrenbacher, Scott

Crosswalk.com is the nation's largest community portal site on the Internet. It is designed to offer a comprehensive range of services such as news, resources, and music as well as community activities like games, forums and chat to its Christian audience. A publicly traded company (symbol AMEN), Crosswalk.com is approaching one million members worldwide.

Folsom, Burton

Burton Folsom is Historian in Residence at the Center for the American Idea in Houston, Texas. He is the author of several books, including The Myth of the Robber Barons, Empire Builders, and Urban Capitalists. The Center can be reached at: 9525 Katy Freeway, Suite 303 Houston, Texas 77024 Phone: (713)984-1343, fax (713)984-0409 or www.americanidea.org.

Griggs, Janella

The Creative Alliance (TCA) is a creative marketing and business development firm near Denver, Colorado. As an integrated marketing agency, TCA is known for their imaginative ideas, effective campaigns and the three "Ps": Positioning, Packaging and Promotion. TCA can be reached at: (888) 293-8101, 102 East Cleveland St. Lafayette, CO 80026, or www.thecreativealliance.com.

Hillman, Os

Workplace Interactive, with Os Hillman as Executive Editor, is a ministry focused on bringing the wisdom of

God into the workplace (www.wowi.net) and founder and director of Marketplace Leaders, an organization designed to mobilize marketplace leaders and their organizations to impact the workplace. For further information, visit his Web site at: www.oshillman.com.

Johnson, Patrick
The Values Investment Forum (VIF), whose president is Patrick Johnson, is a research organization that provides values-based research on stocks and mutual funds to socially conservative institutions, investment advisors and mutual fund companies. For more information call (662) 842-5033 or visit the Web site at www.valuesforum.com.

Kays, Scott
Kays Financial Advisory Corporation is an Atlanta-based money management firm registered with the Securities and Exchange Commission that manages approximately $60 million in clients' portfolios. For more information, call: (770) 951-9110, write: 1640 Powers Ferry Road, Building 30, Suite 200, Marietta, GA 30067 or view their web site at: www.scottkays.com.

Lowe, Peter
Peter Lowe International (PLI) is a not-for-profit organization based in Tampa, Florida, dedicated to making a positive impact on society by helping people of all backgrounds realize their potential for success. For seminar schedules or more information, call: 800-689-6961, write: 8405 Benjamin Road, Tampa, FL 33634, or visit www.peterlowe.org.

Marr, Steve
Steve Marr is President of Masters Builders Management, which provides assistance in improving ministry and business effectiveness, focus, quality of delivery and structure from both a national and international

perspective. His daily radio program, Business Proverbs, goes worldwide. He can be reached at 4740 E. Sunrise Drive Tucson, Arizona 85718, Ph (520) 577-6589 or email: SMWMF@JUNO.COM.

Mason, John

Insight International, founded by John Mason, is an organization dedicated to helping people reach their dreams and fulfill their destiny. For more information, write: John Mason PO Box 54996 Tulsa, OK 74155.

Meyer, Paul J.

Paul J. Meyer and his family own more than 40 companies. For information on SMI-USA's full range of personal development materials, call 1-800-678-7319 or visit the web site at www.smi-usa.com. For information on Creative Education Institute's software programs for students with special needs, call 1-800-234-7319 or visit www.ceilt.com. For information on Summers Mill Retreat and Conference Center, visit www.summersmill.com.

Molitor, Brian D.

Molitor International, with Brian D. Molitor as founder and CEO, is a consulting and training firm that specializes in organizational change and human resource development, serving business, government, industry, healthcare and ministry groups. Molitor International 1550 Collins Lane Midland, Michigan, USA, 48640 E mail: molitor@concentric.net Phone: (517) 832-9730 Fax: (517) 835-9993.

Morley, Patrick

Man in the Mirror, founded by Patrick Morley, desires to help bring a credible offer of the gospel to every man in America. Currently, they provide church-based men's events and retreats to help local churches reach men. For more information, write: Man in the Mirror 154 Wilshire

Blvd., Casselberry, FL 32707, call 407-331-0095 or visit their website at: www.maninthemirror.org.

Noon, Tom

Jubilee Tech International is a company that translates Web sites and software into other languages in order to increase a business' global success. Tom is also on the board of directors for Christianbusiness.com, a start-up with the mission to help Christians in business find others with common interests and needs, learn how to integrate biblical principles into business, and solve businsss problems.

Peacocke, Dennis

The mission of Strategic Christian Services is to pioneer in transforming the world we know into the world God has intended. SCS offers products and hosts conferences that enable men and women to discover and live out their God-given destinies with excellence, thereby strengthening the families, businesses, ministries, and nations that they lead. Call: 800-700-0605, write: P.O. Box 2709 Santa Rosa, CA 95405, or view the web site at: www.gostrategic.org.

Pink, Michael Q.

The Strategic Resource Institute (SRI) specializes in building fully customized, principle-centered, sales coaching programs and helping companies implement them within the context of a well thought-out, strategic plan, resulting in revenue growth. For more information, call: 800-860-7514, email: srilogic@aol.com, write P.O. Box 680365, Franklin, TN 37068 or visit the web site at: www.sellingamongwolves.com.

Ramsey, Dave

The Lampo Group, founded by Dave Ramsey, is a counseling firm created to do bankruptcy avoidance counseling. The Dave Ramsey Show, reaching over 1,000,000 people per day, is a national talk radio show dedicated to answering caller's financial questions. For more information, write: 783 Old Hickory Blvd, Suite 257 West, Brentwood, TN 37027, phone: (615) 371-8881, or visit their web site: www.daveramsey.com.

Ross, Charles

Financial Media Services, Inc. is a company dedicated to teaching principles to managing money. Christian Financial Ministries, Inc. is a non-profit ministry that conducts seminars in churches teaching biblically based principles to managing money. For more information, write: P.O. Box 870928 Stone Mountain, Georgia 30087, phone (770) 413-2258, or email: Chuckr9797@aol.com.

Smith, Darrin

Millionaires United, founded by Darrin Smith, includes athletes, accountants, financial planners, attorneys, and more. Millionaires United offers educational and motivational services to its members, equipping them to make wise long-range decisions, investments, and plans that will positively impact them and their following generations. For more information, call 972-233-9107 or write 4020 McEwen, Suite 105 Dallas, TX 75244.

Stanley, Charles L.

The Compassionate Capitalist, founded by Charles L. Stanley, CFP, ChFC, is a firm that offers Estate Planning, Wealth Management, and investment portfolios screened to eliminate practices generally offensive to conservative Christians. He is a General Securities Principal with Mutual Service Corporation, a registered broker/dealer member NASD/SIPC. 5075 Shoreham Place, Suite 200 San Diego, CA 92122 Phone: (858) 546-9488 Email: CharlesStanley@msn.com.

Wallace, Ken

Ken Wallace, "The Business Pastor," oversees a business and ministry that provides practical spiritual direction for business leaders and their organizations to help them become happier and more profitable. The Ken Wallace Company has offices in Illinois, Toronto and London, England. To contact him, call: (800) 235-5690, or email: kenwallace@businesspastor.com. Their website address is www.businesspastor.com.

Zigarelli, Michael

Regent University is the nation's premier Christian Graduate University, offering masters and doctoral degrees in twenty-two degree programs. Students may also pursue degree programs via the Internet. The eight graduate fields of study offered at Regent University include business, communication, counseling and psychology, divinity, education, government, law, and organizational leadership. View their website at: www.regent.edu.

PROFILES of SUCCESS

Larry Burkett
President, Christian Financial Concepts

Zig Ziglar
Chairman, Ziglar Training Systems

Dick DeVos
President, Amway

John Maxwell
Founder, Injoy

Pat Robertson
Founder, Christian Broadcasting Network

Edwin Louis Cole
President, Christian Men's Network

Bill Armstrong
Former US Senator

And many more stories of successful men who have shaped our heritage

Plus the secrets to real success by these significant authors:
Dr. James Dobson   Guy Carlson
Bob Harrison   Steve Farrar   John Mason
Patrick Morley   Phil Downer   and others

The best of
The Christian Businessman
magazine, Volume One

Edited by Ronnie Belanger & Brian Mast

Daryl Kraft

The
Businessman's
Guide To
Real Success

"*I recommend this book to all employers.*"
—LARRY BURKETT

THE
Christian
EMPLOYEE

ROBERT MATTOX